LOOK-ALIKE, SOUND-ALIKE, NOT-ALIKE WORDS

An Index of Confusables

David Powell

Western New Mexico University
Silver City, New Mexico

UNIVERSITY
PRESS OF
AMERICA

Copyright © 1982 by

University Press of America, Inc.

P.O. Box 19101, Washington, D.C. 20036

Library of Congress Cataloging in Publication Data

Powell, David, 1934-
   Look-alike, sound-alike,   not-alike words.

   1. English language--Homonyms--Indexes.   I. Title.
PE1595.P68   1982   428'.1   81-40715
ISBN 0-8191-2564-4   AACR2
ISBN 0-8191-2565-2 (pbk.)

PREFATORY NOTE

This index is the only comprehensive collection of look-alike, sound-alike confusables in the English language. Having more than five times as many words as any of the longest homonym glossaries ever published, it is also the final authority for locating homonyms.

The familiar homonymic trouble-makers are here in abundance; so too are the unfamiliar, even the bizarre. The thoroughness of selection may be observed by a random examination of the volume. Note, for example, that the word to is not confined to its usual group to-too-two but appears in the group tew-to-too-tui-two; similarly, the combination their-there-they're which is included in the homonym glossary of most grammar texts is superseded here by the group their-there-there're-they're-thir.

The largest grouping of confusables is headed by the word ceras:

> ceras, cereous, ceres, Cereus, cerous,
> cerris, ceruse, cirrous, cirrus,
> scirrhous, scirrhus, Sciurus, series,
> serious, serous, siris

Notes on the format and use of this volume:

Kinds of words included:

1.) Homophones, words that sound alike but are spelled differently. This category constitutes the major portion of words herein; indeed, the word homonym is by popular usage almost synonymous with homophone.
2.) Homographs, those homonyms that are spelled alike but pronounced differently. Homographs are entered in all capital letters and frequently appear without other partners.
3.) Near-homonyms and some family groups whose components may be confusables.

Spelling:

Spelling variants are not considered as
a basis for inclusion; in no more than
a dozen instances, and then only where
variants are in equal use, are variants
listed.

Plurals:

Plurals are entered on two bases:
1) frequency of use and 2) as accommodations for words in a group that
would otherwise have been eliminated
from consideration.

Past participles:

Past participles, like plurals, are
entered on two bases: 1) frequency of
use and 2) as accommodations for words
in a group that would otherwise have
been eliminated from consideration.

Capitals:

Proper nouns are capitalized; where a
word may be either capitalized or in
lower case, it is entered both ways and
separated by a slash mark.

Pronunciation:

Because of the peculiarities of the
English language and of regional dif-
ferences in pronunciation, some few
words may not appear to be confusables.
Seeing a word in its group and studying
pronunciation variants in an unabridged
dictionary will account for the group-
ings in the present work.

Definitions:

Since the purpose of this index is to
locate words subject to confusion with
one another or to satisfy curiosity
about similar-sounding, similar-appear-

ing words, it has no definitions. Glossary definitions can never be as useful as those in the best unabridged dictionaries. The index, then, is a dictionary companion rather than a dictionary.

References and cross-references:

To find a confusable group, look up any word that would likely be in the set. Ignorance of the spelling of a word will not be a difficulty in locating a set. The word that is alphabetically first in its set is the one which serves as the headword for all the other words in the set. Every word is cross-referenced except where it immediately follows the headword of its set.

David Powell
Western New Mexico University

a, ae, eh <u>see</u> <u>also</u> ai
Aachen, ak<u>i</u>n
aar, Aor, are, arr, hour, or, ORE,
    our, r <u>see</u> <u>also</u> aer
Aaron, arrant, arrent, Erin, errand,
    errant
Abadan, Abaddon
abaisse, abase
abater, abator, abattoir
abbacy, abbasi
abbé, abbey <u>see</u> <u>also</u> abe and obeah
abbot, abet
abdominal, abominable
abductor, adductor, eductor
abe, abeigh, obey <u>see</u> <u>also</u> obeah
    <u>and</u> abbé
Abel, abele, able
aberrance, abhorrence
abet <u>see</u> abbot
abeyance, obedience, obeisance
abhorred, aboard, abord
abhorrence <u>see</u> aberrance
abjure, adjure
ablate, ablaut
able <u>see</u> Abel
abnormal, anormal
aboard <u>see</u> abhorred
abode, adobe
abominable <u>see</u> abdominal
abomination, bombination
abord <u>see</u> abhorred
abortin, abortion
ABSENT
absinthin, absinthine
absorb, adsorb
ABSTRACT
ABUSE
Acacian, acaciin, Acadian, Akkadian,
    occasion <u>see</u> <u>also</u> cadjan
Acaena, acana
acanthine, acanthion
acanthous, acanthus/Acanthus
acarid, acrid
accede, axseed, exceed, exede
accedence, accidence, accidens,
    accidents
accelerate, exhilarate
accept, except, expect
acceptable, exceptable

1

accepter, acceptor, accipiter
access, excess
accessary, accessory
accidence see accedence
accidens see accedence
accidents see accedence
accipiter see accepter
accite, excite see also excide
acclaim, exclaim
acclamation, acclimation, exclamation
accomplice, accomplish, complice
accrue, ecru
accusation, acquisition
ace, Ais
acentric, eccentric
acephalous, acephalus
Acer, acier, Aesir see also achor
    and Aissor
acetal, acetol, acetyl
acetic, acidic, aesthetic, ascetic
acetin, acetoin, acetone
acetol see acetal
acetone see acetin
acetyl see acetal
achor, acker, acre see also Acer
acier see Acer
acinous, acinus
acker see achor
acme, acne
acre see achor
acquaint, acquent
acquest, acquiesced, acquist
acquisition see accusation
acquist see acquest
acre see achor
acrid see acarid
acrogenous, acrogynous
acrophobia, agoraphobia
acrose, across
actin, actine, acting, actinine,
    actinon, acton
acts, ax (axe)
ad, add
ada, Adai, adda
Adam, atom
adamant, adhamant
adamantane, adamantine
adapt, adept, adopt
adaptation, adoptian, adoption

add *see* ad
adda *see* ada
adder, attar, atter
ADDICT, adduct, attic
addition, edition
adds, ads, adz (adze)
adduce, educe
adduct *see* addict
adductor *see* abductor
ade, aid, aide
Adelea, Adelia
adenase, adenose
adept *see* adapt
à deux, adieu, adieux, ado, a due
adhamant *see* adamant
adherence, adherents
adherents *see* adherence
adieu *see* à deux
adieux *see* à deux
adjoin, adjourn
adjure *see* abjure
adjutant, agitant
administer, minister
administration, menstruation,
    ministration
ado *see* à deux
adobe *see* abode
adolescence, adolescents
adoors, adores
adopt *see* adapt
adoptian *see* adaptation
adoption *see* adaptation
adores *see* adoors
adrenalin, adrenaline, adrenalone
adroop, adrop
ads *see* adds
adsorb *see* absorb
a due *see* à deux
adulterator, adulterer
adulteress, adulterous
adventuress, adventurous
adverse, avers, averse
advice, advise
advocaat, advocate
adz (adze) *see* adds
ae *see* a
Aegean, Augean
aegis, ages
Aegle, eagle

3

Aeolian, Eolian
aer, air, aire, Ayr, e'er, ere, eyre,
    heir see also aar and aerie
aerial, areal, areole, ariel/Ariel
Aerian, Aryan
aerie, aery, airy, eerie, eery, Eire,
    Erie see also aar and aer
Aeschylus, Aesculus
Aesir see Acer
aesthetic see acetic
aestheticism, asceticism
Aeta, eta/Eta
Aex, Aix, ex, x
afear, affair, affaire, affeer
affect, effect
affectation, affection, affixion
affected, effected
affection see affectation
affective, effective
affeer see afear
afferent, efferent
affidavit, avadavat
affixion see affectation
affluence, effluence
affluent, effluent
afflux, efflux
affreight, affright, afreet
affront, effront
affusion, effusion
afreet see affreight
Africander, Afrikaner
Africans, Afrikaans
Afrikaner see Africander
aftermast, aftermost
agama/Agama, agamae, agamy
AGAPE
agapetae, agapeti
agar, agger
AGATE
AGED
ages see aegis
agger see agar
aggrade, aggrate
aggress, egress
aggressin, aggression, egression
agitant see adjutant
Agnatha, agnathia
agnize, agonize
agon, agony

agonize see agnize
agony see agon
agora, agra/Agra
agoraphobia see acrophobia
agra/Agra see agora
agrapha, agraphia
agreement, agrément
agreements, agrémens
agrees, agrise
agrémens see agreements
agrément see agreement
agrise see agrees
agust, AUGUST, auguste/Auguste
ah, aw, awe
ahl, all, aul, awl, oil
Aht, at, att
ai, ay, aye, eye, I see also a
aid see ade
aide see ade
aiel, AIL, ale see also aisle
aigrette, egret
ail see aiel
aileron, allerion
aims, Ames
ain, ane, eigne see also a and an
ain't, ant, an't, aunt
air see aer
aire see aer
airy see aerie
Ais see ace
aisle, I'll, isle see also aiel
Aissor, icer see also acer
ait, ATE, eight
aiten, eighteen
aition, Idaean, idaein
aiver, aver, ever
Aix see Aex
akin see Aachen
Akkadian see Acacian
aku, ecu
a la, ALA, Allah
a la mode, alamode
alan, aland
alas/Alas, alias
Alascan, Alaskan
alation, elation, illation
albam, album
albas, albus
album see albam
albumen, albumin

5

albus see albas
Alca, Alcae
Alcae see Alca
alcanna, alkanna/Alkanna
alcatras, Alcatraz
Alcatraz see alcatras
alcyon, halcyon/Halcyon
ale see aiel
Alectrion, Alectryon, electron
alee, allay, allée, alley
alegria, alegrias
Alexandrian, Alexandrine
Alexian, alexin
Algerian, Algerine
alias see alas
alight, alite
aliment, element
alimental, elemental
alimentary, elementary
alite see alight
aljama, aljamia
alkanal, alkanol, alkenyl, alkynyl
alkanna/Alkanna see alcanna
alkanol see alkanal
alkenyl see alkanal
alkynyl see alkanal
all see ahl
Allah see a la
allay see alee
allée see alee
allegator, alligator see also allocator
allege, allège
allerion see aileron
alleviate, alluviate, elevate,
    eluviate, illuviate
alleviation, eluviation
alley see alee
alligator see allegator
allision, allusion, elision,
    elusion, Elysian, illusion
alliterate, illiterate
allocator, allocatur see also allegator
allocute, elocute
allocution, elocution
ALLONGE
allophane, allophone
allot, a lot
allowed, aloud
all ready, already
all together, altogether

6

allude, elude, elute, illude
allure, Alur, alure
allusion see allision
allusive, elusive, illusive
alluvial, eluvial, illuvial
alluviate see alleviate
alluvium, eluvium, illuvium
all ways, always
almon, almond
alms, ohms
aloe, halo
a lot see allot
aloud see allowed
already see all ready
altar, alter
altern, alterne
alternat, alternate
alterne see altern
altogether see all together
alumen, illumine
alumna, alumnae, alumni, alumnus
Alur see allure
alure see allure
always see all ways
ama, amah
amaas, amass
amah see ama
amandin, amandine
amass see amaas
ambeer, amber
ambience, ambiens
ameen, amen, amene, amine, ammine
amend, amende, emend
amendation, emendation
amende see amend
amene see ameen
amerce, immerse
Amerind, amyrin
Ames see aims
amice, amiss, remiss
amine see ameen
amiss see amice
amission, emission, omission
amitate, imitate
ammine see ameen
amnesiac, amnesic
amor, amour
Amora, amra
amoral, immoral

amorphous, amorphus
amour *see* amor
amra *see* Amora
amylase, amylose
amyrin *see* Amerind
an, and, ann/Ann *see* *also* a *and* ain
anacrisis, anacrusis
anal, anil, anile, annal, annual
analyst, annalist, annualist
Anchitea, Anchistea
anchor, anker
anchorite, ankerite
and *see* an
androgen, androgyne
androgenous, androgynous
androgeny, androgyny
androgyne *see* androgen
androgynous *see* androgenous
androgyny *see* androgeny
ane *see* ain
anecdotal, antidotal
anecdote, antidote
anesthesia, euthanasia
anestrous, anestrus
anew, anu, enew
angel, angle
anglaise, Anglice
angle *see* angel
Anglian, Anglic, Anglican
Anglice *see* anglaise
angulous, angulus
anhydride, anhydrite
ani, any
anil *see* anal
anile *see* anal
anilide, aniliid
aniliid *see* anilide
animas, animus
anise, anus
anker *see* anchor
ankerite *see* anchorite
ann/Ann *see* an
annal *see* anal
annalist *see* analyst
ANNEX
announce, enounce
annualist *see* analyst
annunciate, enunciate

annual see anal
annualist see analyst
anonym, antonym
anorchous, anorchus
anormal see abnormal
anorthite, anorthitite
Ansar, Anser, answer
ant see ain't
an't see ain't
ante, anti, auntie
antecedence, antecedents
anthranol, anthranoyl
anthropophagous, anthropophagus
anti see ante
antic, antique
antidotal see anecdotal
antidote see anecdote
antimony, antinomy
antique see antic
antonym see anonym
anu see anew
anus see anise
any see ani
anyway, any way
Aor see aar
aoul/Aoul, owl
apar, aper
apart, aport, apport
apatite, appetite
aphagia, aphakia, aphasia
apian, apiin, Appian
apical, epical, epochal
apiin see apian
Apios, apiose
aplomb, aplome
apocalyptic, apocryphal/Apocryphal
apologue, apology, epilogue
aporia, aporrhoea
aport see apart
apostrophe, appositive
apothegm, apothem
Appalachian, appellation, epilation
appellant, appellate
appellation see Appalachian
apperceive, perceive
apperception, perception
appertain, pertain
appetite see apatite

Appian _see_ apian
apport _see_ apart
appose, oppose
apposite, opposite
apposition, opposition
appositive _see_ apostrophe
appraisal, uprisal
appraise, apprise, apprize, praise
apprecate, appreciate
appressed, oppressed
appression, oppression
apprise _see_ appraise
apprize _see_ appraise
APPROPRIATE, expropriate
APPROXIMATE, proximate
appurtenant, pertinent
apteral, apterial
aquate, equate
aquation, equation
Aquilian, aquiline
ara/Ara, aura
Arachnid, arachnoid
araeostyle, araeosystyle
araña, Aranea, Araneae
araneous, Araneus, erroneous
arbiter, orbiter
arc, ARCH, ark, orc
ARCH _see_ arc
archelogy, archeology
arcus, orchis/Orchis
arder, ardor, order, ordure
are _see_ aar
area, aria
areal _see_ aerial
areole _see_ aerial
argal, argil, argol, argyle/Argyle
Argas, argus/Argus
Argentan, argentian, argentine/
    Argentine
argentose, argentous
argil _see_ argal
Argo, argot, ergo, ergot
argol _see_ argal
argon, Oregon, organ, origan, Origen,
    origin, orogen
argot _see_ Argo
argue, orgue
argus/Argus _see_ Argas
argyle/Argyle _see_ argal
aria _see_ area

arid, ariid
ariel/Ariel see aerial
ariid see arid
ark see arc
Amenian, Arminian
armonica, harmonica
arn, iron
arr see aar
arrant see Aaron
arras/Arras, arris, aurous, orris
array, awry
arrect, erect
arrent see Aaron
arris see arras/Arras
ARRIVE
arsine, arson
art, ort
Arthur, author
artis, artiste
Aryan see Aerian
ascent, assent
ascetic see acetic
asceticism see aestheticism
ascot, escot
assai, assay, essay
assart, assert, assort
assay see assai
assent see ascent
assert see assart
assi, assis
assigner, assignor
assis see assi
assistance, assistants
assort see assart
aster/Aster, astir, Astor, astur/
    Astur
astral, austral/Austral
astray, estray
astur/Astur see aster/Aster
at see aht
att see aht
ATE see ait
atom see Adam
attach, attache
attar see adder
attendance, attendants
attenuate, extenuate
atter see adder
attic see addict
ATTRIBUTE

11

audacious, edacious
auetö, auto, otto/Otto
Augean see Aegean
auger, augur
aught, ought see also naught
     under knot
augur see auger
AUGUST see agust
august/August see agust
auguste/Auguste see agust
aul see ahl
aum, oam, ohm, olm, om
aune, awn, on, own
aunt see ain't
auntie see ante
aura see ara
aural, aureole, oral, Orel, oriel,
     oriole see also aerial
aurate, aureate
aureole see aural
aureous, aureus see also arras
auricle, oracle
aurous see arras/Arras
austenite, austinite
austral/Austral see astral
autarchy, autarky
author see Arthur
auto see auetö
autogenetic, autogenic
automation, automaton
autonomous, autonymous
auxin, oxen
avadavat see affidavit
avail, aval, avale
aver see aiver
avers see adverse
averse see adverse
aversion, eversion
avert, evert
avocation, evocation
aw see ah
away, aweigh, way
awe see ah
aweigh see away
awful, offal
awl see ahl
awn see aune
awning, owning
awry see array

ax (axe) see acts
axel/Axel, axial, axil, axle see
     also axile
axes, axis
axial see axel/Axel
axil see axel/Axel
axile, exile see also axel/Axel
axis see axes
axle see axel/Axel
axseed see accede
ay see ai
aye see ai
Ayr see aer
Azrael, Israel

        B

b , be, bee
ba, baa, bah
Baal, bail, bale, bel, bell, belle
babble, Babel
Babi, baby
baboen, baboon
baby see Babi
bacchanal, bacchanale
bacchius, Bacchus
bach/Bach, bache, batch, bauch
bacterin, Bactrian
bad, bade
baddy, batty
bade see bad
baetyl, beadle, bedel, beetle, betel
bag, beg
bah see ba
bahr, bar, Bhar
baht, bahut, bat, batt
bail see Baal
bailee, bailey, bailie, bailli
bain, ban, band, bane, banned
bairn, barn, born, borne, bourn
bait, bate
baiter, bater
baiting, bating
baize, base, BASS, bays, beys
Bakshaish, baksheesh
balaam/Balaam, balam, ballam
balas, ballas
bald, balled, bawled
baldie, baldy

        13

bale see Baal
baleen, balian
ball, baule, Baule, bawl
ballad, ballade, ballet, ballot
ballam see balaam/Balaam
ballas see balas
balled see bald
ballet see ballad
ballon, balloon, balun
ballot see ballad
ballow, balow
ball peen, ball pen
BALLUP
balm, bomb, bombe
balow see ballow
balun see ballon
ban see bain
banc, bank
band, banned see also bain
bandie, bandy
bands, banns, bans
bandy see bandie
bane see bain
bank see banc
banket, banquet, banquette
banned see band and bain
banns see bands
banquet see banket
banquette see banket
bans see bands
bantay, banty
banzai, bonsai
bar see bahr
barat, baratte
barb, barbe
Barbary, barberry, barbery,
    bearberry, burberry
barbe see barb
barbel, barbell
barberry see Barbary
barbery see Barbary
barbet, barbette
bard, barde, barred
bardé, bardee, bardie, bardy
bare, barré, bear see also barit
baren, baron, baronne, barren
bari, barry, berry, bury
baring, bearing, Bering

14

barit, barite, barret, barrette,
    beret see also berate
baritone, baryton, barytone
bark, barque
barn see bairn
baron see baren
baroness, barrenness
baronne see baren
barque see bark
barracouta, barracuda
barré see bare
barred see bard
barrel, barrow
barren see baren
barrenness see baroness
barret see barit
barrette see barit
barrow see barrel
barry see bari
baryton see baritone
barytone see baritone
basal, Basel, basil
base see baize
based, bast, baste
Basel see basal
BASES, basis, basses
basil see basal
basis see bases
bask, basque/Basque
basophil, basophile
basque/Basque see bask
BASS see baize
basses see bases
bast see based
bastaard, bastard
baste see based
bat see baht
batch see bach/Bach
bate see bait
bater see baiter
bath/Bath, bathe
bating see baiting
bats, batts, batz
batt see bat
battel, battle
batterie, battery
battle see battel
batts see bats

battu, battue, batu
batty see baddy
batu see battu
batz see bats
bauble, bobble, bubble
bauch see bach/Bach
bauchle, buckle
baule/Baule see ball
Baumer, baumier
bawl see ball
bawled see bald
bawn, Beaune, bon/Bon, bond, bone,
    Bonn, bonne
bay, bey
bays see baize
bazaar, bizarre
be see b
beach, beech
beacon, becken, beckon
bead, bede/Bede, beed
beadle see baetyl
beal, Bhil, Biel, bill/Bill
bean, been, bein, ben/Ben, bend,
    bin see also bind
bear see bare
bearberry see Barbary
beardie, beardy
bearing see baring
beast, best, beste
beat, beet
beau, bo, BOW
Beaune see bawn
becken see beacon
beckon see beacon
become, becoom
bedder, better, bettor
bede/Bede see bead
bedel see baetyl
bee see b
beebee, Bibby, bibi
beech see beach
beed see bead
been see bean
beer, bier
beery see biri
bees, bise
beet see beat
beetle see baetyl

16

beg see bag
begin, beguin, beguine / Beguine
behoof, behoove
bein see bean
bel see Baal
belay, belie, bely
belga, belgae/Belgae
belie see belay
believe, belive
bell seeBaal
bellboy, bell buoy
belle see Baal
bellow, bellows, below, billow, bilo
belter, Beltir
bely see belay
ben/Ben see bean
bend see bean
bend see bean
benison, venison
benne, benny, binny see also bean
benzal, benzil, benzol, benzoyl,
    benzyl
ber, birr, burr
berat, berate see also barit
beray, bewray
beret see barit
Bergan, Bergen, berghaan
Bering see baring
berley, burley, Burley, burly
Bern, Berne, birn, birne, burn
berry see bari
berth, birth
beryl, birl, burl
beseech, besiege
beside, besides
besiege see beseech
best see beast
beste see beast
beta, betta
betel see baetyl
betta see beta
better see bedder
bettor see bedder
betyl see baetyl
bewray see beray
bey see bay
beys see baize
bezel, bezzle
Bhar see bahr

17

Bhil see beal
bhut, but, butt, butte/Butte
bi, buy, by, bye
bias, bios
bib, bibb
Bibby see beebee
bibi see beebee
bicycle, biocycle
bidder, bitter
bidding, biding, biting
biddy, bitty
biding see bidding
Biel see beal
bield, billed, build
bier see beer
big, bigg
biggen, biggin
bight, bite
bill/Bill see beal
billed see bield
billie/Billie, billy/Billy
billow see bellow
bilo see bellow
billy/Billy see billie/Billie
bin see bean
bind, bine
binny see benny/Benny
biocycle see bicycle
bios see bias
bird, burd, burred, Byrd
birdie, birdy, burdie
biri see beery
birk, burke/Burke
birl see beryl
birma, Burma
birn see Bern
birne see Bern
birr see ber
birth see berth
bise see bees
bison, byzen
bit, bitt
bite see bight
biting see bidding
bitt see bit
bitter see bidder
bitty see biddy
bizarre see bazaar
bladder, blatter

18

blae, blay
blanc, blanch, Blanche, blank, blench
blasé, blaze
blastie, blasty
blat, blate, bleat
blatter see bladder
blay see blae ,
blaze see blasé
bleach, bleech
bleat see blat
bleech see bleach
blench see blanc
blend, blende
blender, blendor
blenny, blini
BLESSED, blest
blew, blue
blight, blite
blini see blenny
blite see blight
blo, blow
bloc, block
blocage, blockage
block see bloc
blockage see blocage
blond, blonde
blore, blower
blow see blo
blower see blore
blue see blew
bluepoint, blue point
bo see beau
boar, boer/Boer, bohor, Bohr, boor,
    bor, bore, BOWER
board, bord, bored
boarder, bordar, border, bordure
bearish, boorish
boat, bote
boatswain, bowssen
bobble see bauble
boce, bos, bose see also boss
bode, BOWED
Boehmian, bohemian/Bohemian
boer/Boer see boar
bogey, bogie, bogy
bohemian/Bohemian see Boehmian
bohor see boar
Bohr see boar
Boii, boy, buoy

bolar, bowler
bold, boled, bolled, bowled
bolder, boulder (bowlder)
bole, boll, bowl
boled see bold
boll see bole
bolled see bold
boltin, Bolton
bomb see balm
bombard, bombarde
Bombay, bomb bay, bombe, bombé
bombination see abomination
bon/Bon see bawn
bond see bawn
bondar, bonder
bonds, bonze
bone see bawn
boney, Boni
Bonn see bawn
bonne see bawn
bonsai see banzai
bonze see bonds
boobie, booby
boo-boo, boubou
booby see boobie
boodie, bootee, booty
boogie, bougie
boon, Boone see also bawn
boor see boar
boorish see boarish
boos, booze
boosy, boozy
bootee see boodie
booty see boodie
booze see boos
boozy see boosy
bor see boar
bord see board
bordar see boarder
border see boarder
bordure see boarder
bore see boar
bored see board
born see bairn
borne, bornee see also bairn
bornee see borne
borough, borrow, burro, burrow
      see also barrel and bureau
bos see boce

20

bose see boce
boss, bosse, bossy see also boce
botany, botonée
bote see boat
botonée see botany
boubou see boo-boo
bouche, bush
bough, BOW see also beau
bougie see boogie
bouillon, bullion
boulder see bolder
BOULE, boulle see also bul
bourdon, burden
bourn see bairn
bourse, burse
bouse, bows, bowse
BOW see bough and beau
BOWED see bode
BOWER see boar
bowl see bole
bowlder see bolder
bowled see bold
bowler see bolar
bows see bouse
bowse see bouse
bowssen see boatswain
bowyer, boyar, boyer
boy see Boii
boyar see bowyer
boyer see bowyer
bracteal, bracteole
brae, braies, bray, brea, brey
brahman/Brahman, brahmin/Brahmin
braid, brayed
braies see brae
brail, braille/Braille
braise, brays, braze
brake, break
bran, brand
brassie, brassy
brassiere, brazier
brassy see brassie
braul, brawl
brava/Brava, brave, bravo
brawl see braul
bray see brae
brayed see braid
brays see braise
braze see braise

21

brazier see brassiere
brea see brae
breach, breech
bread, bred
break see brake
bream, brim
breast, Brest
breath, breathe
bred see bread
brede, breed
bree, Brie
breech see breach
bred see bread
breed see brede
Brest see breast
breton/Breton, Britain, Briton
brevet, brevit
brew, bruh
brewed, brood
brewis, brews, bruise
brey see brae
briar, brier
bridal, bridle
Brie see bree
brief, brieve
brier see briar
brieve see brief
brig, brigue
brigandine, brigantine
brighten, Brighton
brigue see brig
brim see bream
brisk, brisque
bristle, Bristol
Britain see breton/Breton
Briton see breton/Breton
broach, brooch
broncs, Bronx
brooch see broach
brood see brewed
broom, brume
brows, browse
bruh see brew
bruise see brewis
bruit, brut/Brut, brute
brume see broom
brut/Brut see bruit
brute see bruit
bubalis, Bubalus

bubble see bauble
buckie, bucky
buckle see bauchle
bucky see buckie
budda, Buddha
budder, butter
Buddha see budda
buddhi, buddy, butty see also budda
BUFFET
build see bield
Bul, bull see also BOULE
bulbil, bulbul
bulbous, bulbus
bulbul see bulbil
bulbus see bulbous
bulgar/Bulgar, bulger, bulgur
bull see Bul
bullion see bouillon
bunce, bunts
bunion, Bunyan
bunts see bunce
Bunyan see bunion
buoy see Boii
burberry see Barbary
burd see bird
burden see bourdon
burdie see birdie
bureau, buro see also borough
burger, burgher
burke/Burke see birk
burl see beryl
burley/Burley see berley
burly see berley
Burma see birma
burn see Bern
burnie, byrnie
buro see bureau
burro see ber
burred see bird
burro see borough
burrow see borough
burse see bourse
burst, bussed, bust
bury see bari
bus, buss
bush see bouche
business, busyness
buss see bus
bussed see burst

bust _see_ burst
busyness _see_ business
but _see_ bhut
butanal, butanol, butanyl
butein, butene
butt _see_ bhut
butte/Butte _see_ buht
butter _see_ budder
butty _see_ buddhi
buy _see_ bi
buyer, byre
by _see_ bi
bye _see_ bi
Byrd _see_ bird
byre _see_ buyer
byrnie _see_ burnie
Byzantian, Byzantine
byzen _see_ bison

C

c, cee, sea, see, si, Szi
caam, calm
caama, CHAMA, coma, comma, couma,
    kaama
caaming, coming
caapi, coppy, copy
cabal, cable
Cabala, kabbalah
caballer, cavalier, cavaliere, caviler
cabana, cabane, cabin
cabber, caber
cabin _see_ cabana
cable _see_ cabal
cacao, coco, cocoa
caccia, cacha _see also_ cache
cacha _see_ caccia
cache, cash _see also_ caccia
cachou, cashew
cacoon, cocoon
cad, cade _see also_ cade _under_ separate
    listing
caddie, caddy, catty, qadi
caddis, caddish, cattish, kaddish
caddle, cadelle, cattle, katel
Caddo, caddow
caddy _see_ caddie
cade, caid _see also_ cad
cadelle _see_ caddle
cadence, cadency

24

cadge, cage, kedge see also catch
cadger, catcher
cadjan, cajun see also Acacian
caduceus, caducous
caecilian, Sicilian
Caesar, caesura, scissure, seizer,
    seizor, seizure see also cicer
cage see cadge
caid see cade
caiman, caman, Cayman
Cain, cane
caique, cake
caisson, casson, cassone, cassoon
cajun see cadjan
cake see caique
cala, calla/Calla
calaber, calabur, caliber, caliper,
    caliver, coluber/Coluber
calamine, Calymene
Calandra, calandria, Calendra see
    also calendar
calash, caleche, caliche see also clash
calculous, calculus, calyculus
Calderon, caldron
caleche see calash
calendar, calender, calenture see
    also Calandra
calf, CALVE
CALIANA
caliber see calaber
caliche see calash
calico, caligo
calin, caline
caliper see calaber
caliver see calaber
calix, calyx
calk, calque, cauk, caulk, cawk
    see also cock
call, caul, cawl, coil, col, coll,
    cowl, cowle
calla/Calla see cala
called, cauld
caller, choler, collar, collier,
    color, colure, couleur, coulier
callosal, colossal
callose, callous, callus
callow, caló
callus see callose

calm see caam
caló see callow
caloric, choleric
calories, caloris
calot, calotte
calque see calk
calques, calx
Calvary, cavalry
calve see calf
calx see calques
calyculus see calculous
Calymene see calamine
calyptra, calyptratae
calyptratae see calyptra
calyx see calix
camail, camel
caman see caiman
camara, camera, camorra
Cambar, camber
came, kame
camel see camail
cameline, Chamaeleon, chameleon
camera see camara
camise, chemise
camorra see camara
campanile, campanilla, campanula
camp fire, camphire, camphor
camphene, camphine
camphire see camp fire
camphor see camp fire
Campine, campion
Camptosaurus, Camptosorus
can, cann, Cannes, khan
Canada, Kannada
canaille, canal, cannel
canal see canaille
canapé, canopy
canaster, canister (cannister)
canceleer, canceler
cancellous, cancellus
cand, canned
cane see Cain
canister (cannister) see canaster
cann see can
cannable, cannibal
cannel see canaille
canned see cand
Cannes see can

26

cannibal see cannable
cannister see canaster
cannon, cañon, canun, canyon (cañon)
canny, cany
canoa, canoe
canon see cannon
canopy see canape'
cant, can't, Kant, quinte
can't see cant
Cantal, canthal, canticle, cantil, cantle
canter, cantor, kantar
canthal see Cantal
cantharis, cantharus
canticle see Cantal
cantil see Cantal
cantle see Cantal
cantor see canter
canun see cannon
canvas, canvass
cany see canny
canyon (cañon) see cannon
canzon, canzone
caparison, comparison
capelin, capeline
capella, caple, kapelle
CAPER
capital, capitol/Capitol
capitalize, chaptalize
capitaine, capitan, Capsian, captain,
    caption
capitation, captation
capitol/Capitol see capital
caple see capella
caporal, corporal see also corporal
    under separate listing
capot, capote, caput, kaput
cappa see capa
Capparis, caprice
cappie, cappy
caprice see Capparis
caprin, caprine, caproin
caproyl, capryl
Capsian see capitaine
capstan, capstone
captain see capitaine
captation see capitation
caption see capitaine
captor, capture
capuchin, capucine

27

caput see capot
car, carr, caure, coir, kor
carab, caraibe, carib, caribe, carob
carabao, caribou
carabeen, carabin, Cariban, Caribbean
carabineer, carabiner
caracal, caracole, caracul, curricle,
    karakul
caraibe see carab
caramel, cormel
carandá, carandas, caranday, caraunda
carapace, Carapus see also carpus
carat, carate, caret, carotte, carrot,
    karat, karate
caraunda see carandá
carbeen, carbene, carbine, carbon
carbinol, carbinyl, carbonyl
carbon see carbeen
carbonyl see carbinol
carburate, carburet
carcass, caucus, corcass see also
    coccous
carcer, corker see also coarser
    and curser
card, chord, cord, cored
cardanol, cardinal
carding, cording
cardon, cardoon, cordon see also carton
careen, carene
caress, cress
caressed, crest
caret see carat
carey, carry, Cary, kerrie, kerry/
    Kerry see also kerria and corrie
Carian, carrion
carib see carab
Cariban see carabeen
Caribbean see carabeen
caribe see carab
caribou see carabao
caricature, character
caries, carious, Carius, carries
cark, cork/Cork
carlin, carline, carling
carman, carmen/Carmen, carmine
carnate, carnet, cornet, coronate,
    coronet
carny, corney, corny
carob see carab

carol/Carol, carrel
carolin, caroline/Caroline
Carolingian, Carolinian
carom, caroome, Carum
carotid, caryatid
carotte see carat
carousal, carrousel, karrusel
carpal, carpale, carpel
carpus, corpus, karpas see also
    core and carapace
carr see car
carrageen, carrageenin
carrel see carol/Carol
carries see caries
carrion see Carian
carrot see carat
carrousel see carousal
carry see carey
cars, carse see also coarse
cart, carte
carton, cartoon see also cardon
Carum see carom
carvacrol, carvacryl
carvel, carvol
carven, carvene
carvol see carvel
Cary see carey
caryatid see carotid
caryophyllene, caryophyllin
casa, caza
casality, casalty, casualty, causality
casaque, cassock, cossack
cash see cache
cashew see cachou
cask, casque
casket, casquette
casque see cask
casquette see casket
cass, casse
cassation, causation
casse see cass
Cassel, castile/Castile, castle
cassie, cassis, CHASSE, chassis
    see also causus
cassock see casaque
casson see caisson
cassone see caisson
cassoon see caisson
cast, caste
castana, Castanea

caste see cast
castelet, castellate
castellan, castellano, castilian/
    Castilian
castellate see castelet
caster, castor
castile/Castile see Cassel
Castileja, Castilloa
castilian/Castilian see castellan
castle see Cassel
castor see caster
casual, causal
casualty see casality
cat, kat, qat, xat
cataclasm, cataclysm
Catalan, catalin
catch, ketch see also cadge
catcher, see cadger
cate, kate
cathar, cather/Cather
cattish see caddish
cattle see caddle
catty see caddie
caucus see carcass
caudal, caudle, cautel, coddle, cottle
caudex, codex
caudle see caudal
cauf, coff, coif, cough, qoph, quaff
caught, claught
cauk see calk
caul see call
cauld see called
caulicle, caulicole
caulk see calk
caulome, collum, column
caure see car
causal see casual
causality see casality
causation see cassation
cause, causse, caws, chaus
causer, causeur
causse see cause
causus, Cossus see also cassie
cautel see caudal
cautery, cotarii, coterie
cavalier see caballer
cavaliere see caballer
cavalry see Calvary

cavel, cavil
cavernous, cavernulous
cavil see cavel
caviler see caballer
cavvy, cavy
cawk see calk
cawl see call
caws see cause
cay, k, kae, kay, kea, key, quai,
    quay, quey see also qua
Cayman see caiman
caza see casa
cease, cees, seas, sees, seize
cebell, cebil, sibyl/Sibyl
cecil/Cecil, scissel, scissile,
    sisal, sisel, syssel
cedar, ceder, cedor, cedre, seeder
cede, seed
ceder see cedar
cedi, seedy
cedor see cedar
cedre see cedar
cee see c
cees see cease
ceil, ciel, seal, sealed, seel,
    sil, sild, sill see also cell
ceiling, sealing, seeling
ceinture, censer, censor, censure,
    senser, sensor
celebrate, celebret
celery, salary
celesta, celeste/Celeste
celestina, celestine
cell, sail, sale, sel, sell see
    also ceil
cellar, celler, sellar, seller
celtis, celtuce
cembalist, cymbalist, symbolist
cemetery, symmetry
CENACLE
cendre, cinder, sender
cens, cense, cents, scents, sense,
    since
censer see ceinture
censive, sensive
censo, senso
censor see ceinture
censorial, sensorial
censual, sensual

31

censure see ceinture
census, senses
cent, scent, sent
centare, centaur, center, sinter
centaury, centry, century, sentry
center see centare
centry see centaury
cents see cens
century see centaury
cepe, seep, sipe
ceras, cereous, ceres, Cereus, cerous,
    cerris, ceruse, cirrous, cirrus,
    scirrhous, scirrhus, Sciurus,
    series, serious, serous, siris
cerate, cirrate, serate, seriate,
    serrate
Ceratites, Ceratitis
cercal, cercle, circle, Sercial
Cercis, SURCEASE
cercle see cercal
cercus, circus
cere, sear, seer, sere
cereal, seral, serial
cereous, see ceras
ceres see ceras
ceresin, Saracen, sarrazin, sericin
cereus see ceras
ceric, cirque, serac
cerin, cerine, dzeren, serein,
    serene, serin, serine
cero, zero
cerous see ceras
cerris see ceras
cerulean, cerulein
ceruse see ceros
cervical, cervicale
Cervus, service
cesarevich, czarevitch
cesser, sessor
cession, session
cessionary, sessionary
ceston, seston see also sextant
cetaceous, setaceous, psittaceous
cetane, cetene, cetin, seton/Seton
cetyl, setal
cevine, seven
chace, chaise, chase, CHASSE, chez,
    shay, shea see also she and cassie

chack, shack
Chad, shad
chador, chatter
chafe, chaff
chaft, shaft
chagrin, shagreen
chaguar, jaguar see also jaeger
chahar, char
chair, chare, share
chairman, chairmen
chairwoman, chairwomen, charwoman
chaise see chace
chakar, checker, cheka, chekker
chalcedon, chalcedony
chalice, challis
chalybeous, Chalybes
cham, sham
chama see caama
Chamaeleon see cameline
CHAMAR
chameleon see cameline
champagne, champaign/Champaign
CHANA
chanar, channer
chance, chants
chandelle, chandul
changa, chango
channer see chanar
chantecler, chanticleer
chanter, chanteur, chantier
chantey (chanty), shanty
chanteur see chanter
chanticleer see chantecler
chantier see chanter
chanting, tjanting
chants see chance
chanty see chantey
chap, chape, chaps
chapiter, chapter
chaps see chap
chaptalize see capitalize
chapter see chapiter
char see chahar
characin, kerosene
character see caricature
chard, charred, shard
chare see chair
charley/Charley, charlie/Charlie
charpie, sharpie

33

charred see chard
chary, cheery, cherry, shary, sherry
chase see chace
chased, chaste
chaser, chasseur
chasm, chiasm
CHASSE see chace and cassie
chasseur see chaser
chassis see cassie and chace
chaste see chased
chat, chert
chatelain, chatelaine
chatter see chador
chatty, cherty
chaudron, chawdron
chaus see cause
chausses, shows
chawdron see chaudron
chay, chi
cheap, cheep, chip
CHEBEC
chechem, chechen
check, cheque, Czech
checker see chakar
checkoff, check off, Chekov
cheddar, cheder
cheek, chic, chick, sheik, shik
cheeky, chicky, chikee
cheep see cheap
cheery see chary
cheka see chakar
chekker see chaker
Chekov see checkoff
CHELA
chelidonine, chelidonium
chemise see camise
chemosis, chemosmosis
chemotrophic, chemotropic
Chen, chin
chena see chana
cheque see check
cherry see chary
chert see chat
cherty see chatty
chess, chest
chevee, chevet
chewet, chewy
chews, chiaus, choice, choose,
     chose, chouse

chewy see chewet
chez see chace
chi see chay
chiasm see chasm
chiaus see chews
chic see cheek
chick see cheek
chickell, chicle
chicken, shikken
chickery, chicory
chicky see cheeky
chief, chieve
chiel, chil, chill
chieve see chief
chikee see cheeky
chil see chiel
chile/Chile, chili, chilly
Chilo, kilo, Kyloe
chime, chyme
chimera, CHIMERE
chin see Chen
ching, jing
chinse, chintz
chip see cheap
chip away, chippewa/Chippewa
chir, chirr, churr
chiripa/Chiripá, chirpa
chirl, churl
chirp, chirrup
chirpy, chirrupy
chirr see chir
chirrup see chirp
chirrupy see chirpy
chitin, chiton
chivey, chivy
chlor, chlore
chlorin, chlorine, chlorion
chlorogenin, chlorogenine
chock, shock
choice see chews
choir, chore, choreus, chorus, quire
chokey, choky
cholangiolitis, cholangitis
cholate, choleate, collate
choleic, colic
choler see caller
choleric see caloric
choose see chews

35

chopin/Chopin, chopine
choral, chorale, corail, coral, corral
    kraal see also crawl
chord see card
chordal, cordal
chore see choir
chorea, correa/Correa, Korea
choree, coree
choreus see choir
Chorti, cordy, corody
chorus see choir
chose see chews
chott, shot
CHOU, jo, shew, shoe, shoo, shou,
    show, shu
chough, chuff
chouse see chews
chow chow, chowchow
chrism, chrisom
christcross, crisscross
chromaticism, chromatism
chrome, crome
chromite, chromitite
chromogen, chromogene
chronical, chronicle
chrysal, crissal, crizzle, crystal
    see also crestal
chrysanthemin, chrysanthemum
chrysis, crises, crisis, kreis
    see also crasis
chrysocholoris, chrysochlorous
chucker, chukar, chukker
chuff see chough
chukar see chucker
chukker see chucker
chunkey, chunky
churl see chirl
churr see chir
chute, shoot, shut
chyme see chime
cicely, ciselé, Sicily
cicer, sizar, sizer see also Caesar
Ciceronianism, ciceronism
cider, sider
ciel see ceil
Cilicia, silicea
cinder see cendre
cinema, synema
cingle, Senegal, single, zingel
    see also cynical

36

cinnamein, cinnamene, cinnamon
cinque, sank, sink, sync
Circe, searce
circle see cercal
circuiteer, circuiter
circuitry, circuity
circulus, surculus
circus see cercus
cirque see ceric
cirrate see cerate
cirrhosis, sorosis
cirrous see ceras
cirrus see ceras
cisele see cicely
cist, cyst
cite, cyte, sight, site
cither, zither
citrean, citrene, citrine, citrinin,
    citron
citrous, citrus
citrullin, citrulline
citrus see citrous
civilite, civility
clack, claque
cladose, cladous
claimant, clamant
claire, clare
clamant see claimant
clammer, clamor
clan, klan
claque see clack
clare see claire
clarino, clarion, clarone
clash, klatch see also calash
classes, classis
claught, claut, clot, clout see
    also caught
clause, claws
claustral, cloistral
claut see claught
claval, clavel
claver, clavier
clavis, clavus
clawk, clock, cloque
claws see clause
cleave, cleve
cleek, click, clique
clef, cleft
clematis, climatius

clench, clinch
cleric, clerk
cleve see cleave
clew, clue
click see cleek
climacterial, climacteric, climactic,
    climatic
climatius see clematis
climb, clime
clinch see clench
cling, kling
clip, klippe
clique see cleek
clivis, clivus
clock see clawk
cloistral see claustral
cloof, kloof
cloque see clawk
clos, clow see also CLOSE
CLOSE, cloths, clothes see also clos
CLOSER, closure, cloture
clot see claught
cloth, clothe
clothes see CLOSE
cloths see CLOSE
cloture see closer
clout see claught
clow see clos
clue see clew
clysis, clyssus
coachee, coachy
coak, coke, colk
coal, cole, kohl
coaled, cold
coarse, coerce, corse, course
    see also cars
coarser, corsair, courser see also
    carser and curser
coast, cost
coastal, costal
coat, COOT, cot, COTE, kot
coater, coder
coax, coix
coaxal, coaxial, coxal
cobbra, cobra
coccal, cockal, cockle
coccous, coccus see also carcass
cock, coq, coque see also calk
cockal see coccal

```
cockbell, cockbill
cocked, coct
cockle see coccal
cocks, cox/Cox
cockscomb, coxcomb
coco see cacao
cocoa see cacao
cocoon see cacoon
coct see cocked
coda, cota, cotta, kota
coddle see caudal
coddling, codling
coder see coater
codex see caudex
codling see coddling
coerce see coarse
coff see cauf
coffea, coffee
coffer, coiffeur, coiffure, cougher
cognation, cognition, connation
cohabit, cohibit
coif see cauf
coiffeur see coffer
coiffure see coffer
coign, coin, coynye, koine/Koine,
    quoin
coil see call
coin see coign
coir see car
coistrel, custrel
coix see coax
coke see coak
col see call
colation, collation
colature, collator, coloratura
cold see coaled
cole see coal
Coleus, Colias
colic see chollic
colin, colleen, collins/Collins
colk see coak
coll see call
cooperation, corporation, corroboration
collage, college
collate see cholate
collar see caller
collard, collared
collate, COLLECT
collation see colation
```

39

collator see colature
COLLECT see collate
colleen see colin
college see collage
collie, colly, coly
collier see caller
collins see colin
collum see caulome
colly see collie
collyba, collybia
Colombian, columbian, columbin,
    columbine
COLON
colonel, cornel, kernel see also
    coronal
color see caller
coloratura see colorature
colorful, colorific
colorin, coloring
collossal see callosal
coluber/Coluber see calaber
columbian see Colombian
columbin see Colombian
columbine see Colombian
column see caulome
columna, columnea
colure see caller
coly see collie
coma see caama
COMAL
comb, combe, coom, coomb, coombe,
    cwm, kolm see also come
comb-back, comeback
combinate, comminate, comminute
combination, commination, commonition
combe see comb
COMBINE
come, cum see also comb
comeback see comb-back
comedic, cometic, comic
comely, cumbly
comer, cumber, cummer
cometic see comedic
comfit, comfort
comfiture, confiture
comfort see comfit
comic see comedic
coming see caaming

comital, comitial
comity, committee
comitial see comital
comma see caama
commence, comments
commendator, commentator, commutator
commendatory, comminatory
commentator see commendator
comments see commence
commerce, commers
commies, commis
commination see combination
comminate see combinate
comminute see combinate
comminatory see commendatory
commis see commies
commissaire, commissar
commissariat, commissariot
commissionaire, commissioner
committee see comity
common, COMMUNE
commonition see combination
COMMUNE see common
commutator see commentator
COMPACT
company, compony
comparable, comparative
comparably, comparatively
comparative, comparable
comparatively see comparably
compare, compear, compeer, compere
comparison see caparison
compass, compesce
COMPASSIONATE
compear see compare
compeer see compare
compere see compare
compesce see compass
complacence, complaisance
complacent, complaisant
complain, compline
complainant, complanate
complaisance see complacence
complaisant see complacent
complanate see complainant
complected, complexioned
complement, compliment
complementary, complimentary

41

complexioned see complected
complice see accomplice
compliment see complement
compline see complain
complimentary see complementary
compony see company
composed, compost
composer, composure
compost see composed
composure see composer
compotation, computation
COMPOUND
COMPRESS
compressor, compressure
compromis, compromise
compter, contour, counter, countour
comptroller, controller
compulsive, compulsory
computation see compotation
comrade, kamerad
con, conn
conation, connotation
conative, connotative
CONCATENATE
concent, consent
CONCERT
CONCHA
conciliable, conciliabule
CONCINNATE, consonant
CONCORD
concordant, concordat
concours, concourse
CONCRETE
concur, conker, conquer
cond, conned
condemn, contemn
condemner, contemner
conduce, CONDUCT
CONFECT
confectionary, confectionery
confidant, confidante, confident,
    confitent
confidantes, confidants, confidence
confident see confidant
confidentially, confidently
CONFINE
confirm, conform
confirmation, conformation
confitent see confidant

confiture see comfiture
CONFIATE
conform see confirm
conformation see confirmation
confrere, confrerie
Confucian, confusion
conga, congé, congee, congo/Congo,
    congou, Kongo
congaree, congeree, congery, congiary,
    conjury
congé see conga
congee see conga
conger, CONJURE see also conga
congeree see congaree
congery see congaree
CONGEST
congiary see congaree
congo/Congo see conga
congou see conga
CONGREGATE
CONGRESS
conic, conical, conicle
CONJURE see conger
conjury see congaree
conker see concur
conn see con
connate, connote
connation see cognation
connects, CONNEX
conned see cond
CONNEX see connects
connotation see conation
connotative see conative
connote see connate
conquer see concur
conscience, conscious
CONSCRIPT
consent see concent
consequence, consequents
conservatoire, conservator
CONSERVE
consistently, constantly
CONSOCIATE
consol, CONSOLE, consul, council,
    counsel
consommé, consume
consonance, consonants
consonant see concinnate

consonants _see_ consonance
CONSORT
constance, constants
constant, constat
constantly _see_ consistently
constants _see_ constance
constat _see_ constant
CONSTRUCT
consul _see_ consol
consulter, consultor,
consume _see_ consomme
contact, CONTRACT
CONTE
contemn _see_ condemn
contemner _see_ condemner
CONTENT
contentation, contention
CONTEST
contingence, contingency
continual, continuous
continuant, CONTINUATE
continuous _see_ continual
contour _see_ compter
CONTRACT _see_ contact
controller _see_ comptroller
controversal, controversial
convect, CONVICT
convects, convex, CONVICTS
CONVENT
conventical, conventicle
CONVERSE
CONVERT
converter, convertor
convex _see_ convects
CONVICT _see_ convect
CONVICTS _see_ convects
coo, COUP, cue, Kew, q, queue
    see _also_ coop
cookie, Kuki
coolamon, Kulaman
coolie, coolly, cooly, coulé, coulee
coolies, coulisse
coolly _see_ coolie
coom _see_ comb
coomb _see_ comb
coombe _see_ comb
coop, COUP, COUPE, cupay _see_ _also_ coo
cooper/Cooper, COUPER, kupper

co-operate, CORPORATE
cooperation, corporation, corroboration
coot see coat
COOTER
COOTIE, coudé
copa, coppa
copaene, copain
copies, coppice, cops, copse
coppa see copa
coppice see copies
coppy see caapi
cops see copies
copse see copies
copy see caapi
copyright, copywrite
coq see cock
coque see cock
coquet, coquette see also crochet
corail see choral
coral see choral
corbeil, corbel
CORBIE, karbi
corcass see carcass and coccous
cord see card
cordal see chordal
cording see carding
cordon see cardon
cordy see Chorti
core, corps see also carpus and
    carapace
cored see card
coree see choree
corespondent, correspondent
corial, correal
cork see cark
corker see carcer
cormel see caramel
cormose, cormus
cornada, coronado/Coronado
cornel see colonel
corner, coroner
cornet see carnate
corney see carny
corn flour, cornflower
cornice, cornus, coronis
corny see carny
corody see Chorti
corollate, correlate

45

corona, crone, crony, korona, koruna,
    krona, krone
coronado/Coronado see cornada
coronal, coronale see also colonel
coronate see carnate
coroner see corner
coronet see carnate
coronis see cornice
corporal, corporeal see also caporal
corporate see co-operate
corporation see co-operation
    (cooperation)
corporeal see corporal
corps see core
corpse see core
corpus see carpus
corral see choral
correa/Correa see chorea
correal see corial
correlate see corollate
correspondence, correspondents
correspondent see corespondent
correspondents see correspondence
corrida, corrido, courida
corrie, courie, cowrie, kauri
corroboration see cooperation
corsair see coarser
corse see coarse
corte, court
cortes, Cortez, courts
Cortez see cortes
corydalis, corydalus
corypha, coryphaeus, coryphée
cos, cose
coscet, cosset, cossette, cossid
cose see cos
cosher, kosher
cosine, cousin, cozen, kosin
cossack see casaque
cosset see coscet
cossette see coscet
cossid see coscet
Cossus see causus
cost see coast
costal see coastal
costard, custard
costmary, customary
cot, cotte see also coat
cota see coda
cotarii see cautery

COTE see coat
coteau, coto, koto
coterell, cotterel, cottrell
coterie see cautery
coto see coteau
cotta see coda
cottar, cotter, cottier
cotte see cot
cotter see cottar
cotterel see coterell
cottier see cottar
cottle see caudal
cottrell see coterell
couac, quack
couch, couché, couchee, couchy
coude see cootie
cough see cauf
cougher see coffer
coule see coolie
coulee see coolie
coulette, culet, cullet, culotte
couleur see caller
coulier see caller
coulisse see coolies
couma see caama
coumaran, coumarin
council see consol
councilor, counselor
counsel see consol
counselor see councilor
counter see compter
counterpoise, counterpose
counterpuncher, counterpuncture
countour see compter
countryman, countrymen
countrywoman, countrywomen
COUP see coop and coo
COUPE see coop
couper see cooper/Cooper
couple, cupel, cupule
COURANT, courante see also currant
courb, courbe, curb
courida see corrida
courie see corrie
courier, currier
course see coarse
courser see coarser
court see corte
courter, courtier

47

courtesy, courtoisie
courtier see courter
courtoisie see courtesy
courts see cortes
cous, cows
cousin see cosine
coutel, coutil
couture, culture, kultur, kulture
couvert, couverte
coven, covin
covered, covert
covetise, covetous
COVEY
covin see coven
cowan, coween
coward, cowered
coween see cowan
cowered see coward
cowl see call
cowle see call
cowrie see corrie
cows see cous
cox see cocks
coxal see coaxal
coxcomb see cockscomb
coynye see coign
cozen see cosine
crabber, crabbier, crabier
cracking, kraken
cracks, crax, crex
crake, creagh, creaght see also
    creak
cram, crambe, crame
crampette, crampit
cran, crane, kran
cranage, crannage
crance, crants, krantz
crane see cran
craniad, craniate, crannied
cranic, crannock, crannog
crannage see cranage
crannied see craniad
crannock see cranic
crannog see cranic
crants see crance
crape, creep, crepe
crappie, crappy see also crapy
crapy, crepey see also crappie
crasis, krasis see also chrysis

crate, Crete <u>see</u> <u>also</u> creat
crater, krater
craton, kraton
craunch, crunch
crawk, crock
crawl, kraal <u>see</u> <u>also</u> choral
crawley, crawlie, crawly
crax <u>see</u> cracks
crays, craze
crazy, Crécy
creagh <u>see</u> crake
creaght <u>see</u> crake
creak, creek, crick <u>see</u> <u>also</u> crake
cream, creem, crème
creamery, crémerie
crease, crise, criss, kris
creat, CREATE <u>see</u> <u>also</u> crate
creature, critter
Crécy <u>see</u> crazy
creek <u>see</u> creak
creel, krill
creem <u>see</u> cream
creep <u>see</u> crape
creepie, creepy
crème <u>see</u> cream
crémerie <u>see</u> creamery
crenel, crinal
crenelet, crenellate
creole/Creole, criollo
crepe <u>see</u> crape
crepey <u>see</u> crapy
crescent, cresson
cress <u>see</u> caress
cresson <u>see</u> crescent
crest <u>see</u> caressed
crestal, cresyl <u>see</u> <u>also</u> chrysal
Cretan, cretin, cretonne
Crete <u>see</u> crate
cretin <u>see</u> Cretan
cretonne <u>see</u> Cretan
crevasse, crevice
crew, cru, crue, kroo, kru
crewel, crool, cruel
crewer, cruor
crews, crouse, cruise, cruse
crex <u>see</u> cracks
cribble, criblé
crick <u>see</u> creak
Crimean, crimen

49

crinal see crenel
cringle, crinkle
criollo see Creole
crise see crease
crises see chrysis
crisis see chrysis
crispen, crispin
criss see crease
crissal see chrysal
crisscross see christcross
critic, critique
critter see creature
crizzle see chrysal
cro, crow
croatan, Croation, crotin, croton
    see also crocean
crocean, crocin see also croatan
crochet, crocket, croquet, croquette
crocin see crocean
crock see crawk
crocket see crochet
crocus, croquis
CROISE
crome see chrome
crone see corona
crony see corona
crool see crewel
croon, kroon
croquet see crochet
croquette see crochet
croquis see crocus
crosier, crozer
cross, crosse
crossword, crosswort
crotal, crottels, crottle, crotyl
crotin see croatan
croton see croatan
crottels see crotal
crottle see crotal
crotyl see crotal
crouse see crews
crow see cro
crown wart, crownwort
crows, croze
crozer see crosier
cru see crew
crucks, crux
crue see crew
cruel see crewel

cruise see crews
crumby, crummie
crunch see craunch
cruor see crewer
cruse see crews
crush, kurus
crux see crucks
cryptococcosis, cryptococcus
crystal see chrysal
crystallin, crystalline
ctene, teen
cuadrilla, quadrel, quadrille
cuba/Cuba, kuba
cubical, cubicle
cubital, cubitale
cuckhold, cuckold
cuckoo, kuku
cuddle, cuittle, cuttle
cue see coo
cueca, cuica
cuisse, quis, quiz
cuit, cute
cuittle see cuddle
cuivré, quivery
culet see coulette
cullet see coulette
cully, Kulli
culotte see coulette
culture see couture
cum see come
cumber see comer
cumbly see comely
cumene, cumin
cumenyl, cuminol, cuminyl
cumin see cumene
cuminol see cumenyl
cuminyl see cumenyl
cummer see comer
cumol, cumoyl, cumyl
cumulose, cumulous, cumulus
cumyl see cumol
cunette, cunit
cupay see coop
cupel see couple
cupreine, cuprene
cupule see couple
cur, curr
curacao, curassow
curb see courb

curd, Kurd
curdle, curtail, curtal, curtle, kirtle
CURE, Curie, curry, Kure, kurrie
curete, curette
curia, curio
curial, curule, kurrol
Curie see CURE
curine, Kyurin
curio see curia
curios, curious
curn, kern
curr see cur
currack, curragh, Kurukh
currant, current see also courant
currawong, kurrajong
current see currant
curricle see caracal
currier see courier
currish see qursh
curry see CURE
curser, cursor see also corsair
    and carcer
curses, cursus
cursor see curser
cursus see curses
curtail see curdle
curtal see curdle
curtle see curdle
curule see curial
curve, kirve
custard see costard
customary see costmary
custrel see coistrel
cute see cuit
cutler, cuttler
cutter, kuttar
cuttle see cuddle
cuttler see cutler
cwm see comb
cyan, cyon, scion, sign, sine,
    Sion, syne, Zion
cyanide, cyanite, syenite
cyanin, cyanine
cyanite see cyanide
cyclamen, cyclamin, cyclamine
cyclas, cyclus
cycle, psychal see also secle
cycloalkane, cycloalkene

cyclohexane, cyclohexene
cyclopentane, cyclopentene
Cyclopes, Cyclops
cyclophorase, cyclophorus
Cyclops see Cyclopes
cyclus see cyclas
cygnet, signate, signet
cyma, sima
cymbal, symbol
cymbalist see cembalist
cynical, scenical, Senegal see
    also cingle
cynicism, Sinicism
cynocephalous, cynocephalus
cyon see cyan
Cyperus, cy pres, cypress, Cypris,
    Cyprus
cyprian, cyprine
Cypris see Cyperus
Cyprus see Cyperus
cyst see cist
cysteine, cystine, Sistine
cyte see cite
czar, Saar
czarevitch see cesarevich
Czech see check

D

d, dee
da, dah
Dacca, dacha see also dagga
dace, days, daze see also dais
dacha see Dacca
dacian, dation
dacron, dacryon
dactylis, dactylous, dactylus
dad, dade, dead
dae, day, DEY, dhai
daedel, daidle, datal, datil,
    daytale
daemon, daimen, daimon, daman, damen,
    damine, Damon, demon
daeva, deva, diva
daff, daft
dag, dog, doge
dagga, dagger, Daghur see also Dacca
dah see da
daidle see daedel

53

daily, dalea see also dalli
daim, dame see also dam
daimen see daemon
daimon see daemon
daiquiri, dichoree
dairy, derry, diary, dieri
dais, dice, dies see also dace
daisy, desi
dak, doc, dock
Dakar, daker, dekar
dale, del, dell
dalea see daily
daler, dollar, dolor
dales, dells
dallas/Dallas, dalles
dalli, dally see also daily
dam, damn see also daim
daman see daemon
dame see daim
damen see daemon
damewort, danewort
damine see daemon
dammar, dammer
damn see dam
Damon see daemon
dancer, danseur
Dane, deign
danewort see damewort
danglin, dangling
Dannebrog, Donnybrook
dannock, dunnock
danseur see dancer
danta, dante/Dante
dar, daur
darcy, Darzi, D'Orsay
dart, dort
Darzi see darcy
datal see daedel
datil see daedel
dation see dacion
daub, daube
daughter, dodder, dorter, dotter
Dauphin, Dauphine, dolphin
daur see dar
dauw, daw
dawdle, doddle, dottle
day see dae
days see dace
daytale see daedel

54

daze see dace
deacon, decan, decane, deccan, dekan
dead see dad
deal, deil, dele, diel, dill see
    also dial
dean, DENE
dear, deer
deas, dix
deasil, diesel/Diesel
debel, debile
debutant, debutante see also dubitant
decal, deckle
decan see deacon
decane see deacon
deccan see deacon
decease, disease, disseise
deceit, disseat
December, decemvir
decent, descent, dissent
decern, discern
decision, desition
deck, decke
deckle see decal
decollate, décolleté
decompose, discompose
decry, descry
deduce, deduct, diduce
deduced, deducted
deduct see deduce
deducted see deduced
dee see d
deem, deme, diem
deer see dear
defalcate, defecate
defalcation, defecation
defecate see defalcate
defecation see defalcation
defer, differ
deference, deferents, difference
defi, defy
deform, difform
defract, diffract
defy see defi
defuse, DIFFUSE
defuser, diffuser
defusion, diffusion
Dehwar, Dewar, dewer
deign see Dane
deil see deal

dekan see deacon
dekar see Dakar
del see dale
dele see deal
DELEGATE
DELIBERATE
dell see dale
dells see dales
Delphian, Delphin, delphine
delusion, dilution
demarch, demarche
deme see deem
demean, demesne see also bemean
demon see daemon
demonic, demotic
demur, demure
den, din
denature, disnature
DENE see dean
dengue, dinghy, dingy
DENIER, dernier
dense, dents
dent, dint
dental, dentelle, dentil
dentation, dentition
dentelle see dental
denticle, denticule
dentil see dental
dentition see dentation
dents see dense
dependant, dependent
dependence, dependents
dependent see dependant
dependents see dependence
deposal, disposal
depositary, depository
depravation, deprivation
deprecate, depreciate
deprecatory, depreciatory
depreciate see deprecate
depreciatory see deprecatory
deprivation see depravation
derangement, disarrangement
derange, disarrange
dern, durn
dernier see DENIER
derry see dairy
descendant, descendent

descension, dissension see also decent
descent see decent
descry see decry
Deseret, DESERT, dessert, dissert
deserve, disserve
desi see daisy
desition see decision
desman, desmine
desperate, disparate
dessert see Deseret
dessous, dessus
destain, disdain, distain
detent, détente
deter, detur
determinant, DETERMINATE
deterrence, deterrents
detract, detrect
detur see deter
detirb, disturb
deuce, douce, duce
deva see daeva
deval, devel, devil
devalue, disvalue
devel see deval
device, devise
devil see deval
devise see device
deviser, devisor, divisor
devoir, devour see also diver
dew, DO, doo, due see also DO
    under separate listing
Dewar see Dehwar
dewer see Dehwar
dexterous, dextrose
DEY see dae
dhai see dae
dhal, doll see also dhole
dhan, don
dharana, dharna
dhole, dol, dole see also dhal
dhoon, doon, dune see also done
dhoti, doty, doughty
dhow, DOW, tao see also tau
dhyana, diana/Diana
diaeresis, diuresis
diagram, digram
dial, diel, diol see also deal
    and deval
dialectal, dialectical

57

diamine, diamond
diana/Diana see dhyana
diaper, diapir
diary see dairy
dice see dais
dichoree see daiquiri
diction, dition
diduce see deduce
die, dye
died, dyed
diel see deal
diem see deem
dieri see dairy
dies see dais
diesel/Diesel see deasil
diestrous, diestrus
dietetic, dietic
differ see defer
difference see deference
diffide, divide
difform see deform
diffract see defract
DIFFUSE see defuse
diffuser see defuser
diffusion see defusion
DIGEST
dight, dit, dite
digram see diagram
diker, duiker
dilatation, dilation
dill see deal
dilution see delusion
dime, disme
din see den
dinar, diner, dinner
dine, dyne
diner see dinar
dinghy see dengue
dingy see dengue
dining, dinning
dinner see dinar
dinning see dining
dint see dent
diol see dial
diphenol, diphenyl
diphylla, diphylleia
dipterocarpous, dipterocarpus
dipteros, dipterous, dipterus
dire, dyer

58

directoire, director
directress, directrice
dirhem, Durham
disarrange _see_ derange
disarrangement _see_ derangement
disassemble, dissemble
disburse, disperse
disc, disk
discern _see_ decern
discomfit, discomfort
discompose _see_ decompose
DISCOURSE
discoursive, discursive, discussive
discous, discus, discuss
discovered, discovert
discreet, discrete
discriminant, DISCRIMINATE
discursive _see_ discoursive
discus _see_ discous
discuss _see_ discous
discussed, disgust _see also_ discous
discussive _see_ discoursive
disdain _see_ destain
disease _see_ decease
diseur, disour
diseuse, disuse
disgust _see_ discussed
disinfect, disinfest
disjunctor, disjuncture
disk _see_ disc
disme _see_ dime
disnature _see_ denature
disour _see_ diseur
disparate _see_ desperate
disperse _see_ disburse
disposal _see_ deposal
disseat _see_ deceit
disseise _see_ decease
dissemble _see_ disassemble
disseminate, dissimulate
dissension _see_ descension
dissent _see_ decent
dissert _see_ Deseret
disserve _see_ deserve
dissidence, dissidents
dissimilation, dissimulation
dissimulate _see_ disseminate
dissimulation _see_ dissimilation
DISSOCIATE

59

distain see destain
distal, distale
distant, distend, distent
distrait, distraite, distraught
disturb see deturb
disuse see diseuse
disvalue see devalue
dit see dight
dite see dight
dition see diction
diuresis see diaeresis
diva see daeva
diver, dyvour see also devoir
divers, diverse
divertisement, divertissement
DIVES
divide see diffide
divisor see deviser
dix see deas
dizain, dizen see also docent
djin, gin, jen, jin
DO, doe, dough see also dew
doc see dak
docent, doesn't, douzaine, dozen
    see also dizain
docile, dossal
dock see dak
dodder see daughter
doddle see dawdle
doe see DO and dew
DOES, doze
doesn't see docent
dog see dag
doge see dag
doily, dolly
dol see dhole
dole see dhole
doll see dhal
dollar see daler
dollop, doll up
dolly see doily
dollyman, dolman, dolmen
dolor see daler
dolosse, dolose
dolphin see Dauphin
dom, dome
domical, domicile
dominance, dominants
don see dhan

60

dona, doña, donah, donna, donné,
    donnée
done, dun see also dhoon
donjon, dungeon, dungon
donna see dona
donné see dona
donnée see dona
Donnybrook see Dannebrog
doo see dew and DO
dooly, duly
doom, doume
doon see dhoon
door, dor, douar, duar
Doras, Doris, dors, dorse
doré, dory
Doris see Doras
dors see Doras
D'Orsay see darcy
dorse see Doras
dort see dart
dorter see daughter
dory see dore
dossal see docile
dosser, dossier
dost, dust
dotter see daughter
dottle see dawdle
doty see dhoti
douar see door
DOUBLER, doublure
doublet, doublette
doublure see doubler
doubt, dout
doubter, douter
douc, duck see also ducked
douce see deuce
dough see DO and dew
doughty see dhoti
doume see doom
dour, dower
douser, dowser
dout see doubt
douter see doubter
douzaine see docent
DOVE
DOW see dhow
dowager, dowitcher
dowel, dowl

dower see dour/dowitcher see dowager
dowl see dowel
dowser see douser
doyen, doyenne
doze see DOES
dozen see docent
drabby, drabi
drachm, dram, drame
draff, draft, draught see also drought
dragon, dragoon
dram see drachm
drame see drachm
draught see draff
drawbridge, draw bridge
drias, dryas
drog, drogue
droop, drupe
drought, drouth see also draff
drug, drugg
drupe see droop
druse, Druze
dryas see drias
dual, duel
duar see door
dubitant, dubitante see also debutant
duce see deuce
duchess, duchesse
duchy, dutchy
duck see douc
ducked, duct see also douc
ducks, dux
duct see ducked
dudeen, dudine
due see dew and DO
duel see dual
duffel, duffle
duiker see diker
duly see dooly
dun see done
dune see dhoon
dungeon see donjon
dungon see donjon
dunnock see dannock
dur, dure
dural, duryl
dure see dur
Durham see dirhem
durn see dern
duryl see dural

dust see dost
dutchy see duchy
dux see ducks
dye see die
dyed see died
dyeing, dying
dyer see dire
dying see dyeing
dyne see dine
dysphagia, dysphasia
dyvour see diver
dzeren see cerin

E

each, eche
eager, eagre
eagle see aegle
eagre see eager
ear, e'er, ere, err, Iyar see also aer
earing, earring
earl marischal, earl marshal
earn, erne, urn
earnest/Earnest, Ernest
earring see earing
eas, ease
eaten, Eton
eau, o, oe, oh, ow, owe
eave, eve/Eve
eaves, eves
eccentric see acentric
échappé, échappée, echoppe
eche see each
echinococcosis, echinococcus
echoppe see échappé
eclipses, eclipsis
ecru see accrue
ectocarpous, ectocarpus
ecu see aku
ecuelle, equal
edacious see audacious
Edam, Edom
edition see addition
Edom see Edam
educe see adduce
eductor see adductor
Edwardean, Edwardian
eek, eke

eel, ill
e'er see ear
eerie see aerie
eery see aerie
EFFACE
effect see affect
effected see affected
effecter, effector
effective see affective
effector see effecter
efferent see afferent
effete, ephete
effluence see affluence
effluent see affluent
efflux see afflux
effront see affront
EFFUSE
effusion see affusion
eggar, egger
egress see aggress
egression see aggressin
egret see aigrette
eh see a
eight see ait
eighteen see aiten
eigne see ain
Eire see aer and aerie
either, ether
ejaculate, jaculate
eke see eek
el, ell, l
ELABORATE
élan, eland see also eloign
elaps, elapse, illapse
elation see alation
electron see alectrion
elegant, elegante
elegiast, elegist
elegy, elogy
element see aliment
elemental see alimental
elementary see alimentary
elevate see alleviate
eleven, elevon
elicit, illicit
elide, elite, illite
eliminate, illuminate
elision see allision

elite see elide
ell see el
ellipses, ellipsis
elocute see allocute
elocution see allocution
elogy see elegy
eloign, elon see also élan
elude see allude
elusion see allision
elusive see allusive
elusory, illusory
elute see allude
eluvial see alluvial
eluviate see alleviate
eluviation see alleviation
eluvium see alluvium
Elysian see allision
em, I'm, m
emanant, emanate, eminent,
    immanent, imminent
eminence, immanence, imminence
emancipate, mancipate
emancipation, mancipation
emane, immane
emend see amend
emendation see amendation
emerge, immerge
emersed, immersed
emersion, immersion
emigrant, immigrant
emigration, immigration
eminent see emanant
emir, ymir
emission see amission
emit, emmet, immit, omit
emphases, emphasis
emplacement, implacement
emplastic, implastic
empress, emprise, IMPRESS
empyreal, imperial
emulate, immolate
emulation, immolation
en, end, in, Ind, inn, n
enactor, enacture
enarm, enarme
enate, innate
encase, in case
enclose, inclose
end see en

65

endarch, endark
endorse, indorse, indoors
enervate, innervate
en face, enface
England, englyn
enew see anew
enhydros, enhydrous
enounce see announce
ENOW
enplane, en plein
enroot, en route
ens, ense
ensample, ensemble, example, sample
ense see ens
ensemble see ensample
ensign, insigne
ensure, insure
enter, inner, inter
entomology, etymology
ENTRANCE, entrants
entrant, intrant
entrants see ENTRANCE
entree, entry
enumerable, innumerable
enunciate see annunciate
envelop, envelope
envious, invious
envoi, envoy
Eolian see Aeolian
épée, épi
ephemeris, ephemerous
ephete see effete
épi see épée
epic, epoch, epoche
epical see apical
epigram, epigramme
epilation see Appalachian
epilogue see apologue
episodic, epizootic
epistasis, epistaxis, epitasis
epistolar, epistoler
epizootic see episodic
epoch see epic
epochal see apical
epoche see epic
equal see ecuelle
equate see aquate
equation see aquation
equivalence, equivalents

66

erasable, irascible
ere see ear and aer
erect see arrect
ergo see Argo
ergot see Argo
eric/Eric, eruc, Eryx
Erie see aerie
Erin see Aaron
erk, irk
erne see earn
Ernest see earnest/Earnest
eros/Eros, erose
erotic, erratic
err, ur/Ur see also ear and aer
errand see Aaron
errant see Aaron
erratic see erotic
erred, urd
erroneous see araneous
errs, ers, erse
eruc see eric/Eric
erupt, irrupt
eruption, irruption
eruptive, irruptive
Eryx see eric/Eric
eschatological, scatological
escalade, escalate
escot see ascot
esoteric, exoteric
esprit, spirit see also spirit under
    separate listing
ess, esse, s
essay see assai
esse see ess
Esther, ester
ESTIMATE
estray see astray
estrous, estrus
eta see Aeta
Ethel, ethyl
ether see either
ethyl see Ethel
Eton see eaton
etymology see entomology
euphemism, Euphuism
euphrasia, euphrasy
Euphuism see euphemism
euthanasia see anesthesia
eve/Eve see eave

ever, every see also aiver
eversion see aversion
evert see avert
every see ever
eves see eaves
evocation see avocation
ewe, u, yew, you, Yueh
ewer, your, you're
ewes, ouse, USE, yews
ex see Aex
exacerbate, exasperate
exaltation, exultation
examen, examine
example see ensample
exasperate see exacerbate and
    aggravate
exceed see accede
except see accept
exceptable see acceptable
exceptionable, exceptional
excess see access
excide, excite, exite see also
    accite
exciter, excitor
exclaim see acclaim
exclamation see acclamation
EXCUSE
excyst, exist
executer, executor
exede see accede
exercise, exorcise
exert, exhort, exsert
exhilarate see accelerate
exhort see exert
exile see axile
exine, exon
exist see excyst
exite see excide
exitus, exodus/Exodus
exon see exine
exorcise see exercise
exoteric see esoteric
expect see accept
expedience, expedients
EXPLOIT
EXPORT
EXPOSE
expropriate see appropriate
exsert see exert

extant, extent, extinct
extends, extense, extents
extenser, extensor
extent see extant
extents see extends
extenuate see attenuate
extinct see extant
EXTRACT
exude, exute
exultation see exaltation
exute see exude
eye see ai
eyelet, islet
eyre see aer
eyrie see aerie

F

fables, faiblesse
face, fays, faze, feys, fez, phase
    see also faces
faces, facies, fasces, fauces, fazes,
    feces, phases, phasis see also face
facet, fascet, faucet, fassaite,
    fassette see also faucet under
    separate heading
facial, fascial, fetial
facies see faces
facilitate see felicitate
facon, faconne, falcon
factitial, factious, factitious,
    fictitious see also factitive
factitive, factive, factual see also
    factitial
factor, facture
factual see factitive
facture see factor
faddish, fattish, fetish
Faerose, faros, pharoahs, pharos/Pharos
faerie, faery, fairy, feirie, ferry
fagin/Fagin, fagine
fagot, fagott
faiblesse see fables
faik, fake
fail, faille see also file
fain, fan, fane, feign
faint, feint
fair, fare, phare see also far
    and fore

fairy see faerie
fait, fate, fete, fiat see also feat
fake see faik
faker, fakir
falcon see facon
fallow, fella, fellah, feller,
    felloe, fellow, felly
false, faults
familial, familiar
fan see fain
fancy bread, fancy-bred
fandangle, fandango
fane see fain
far, for see also fair and fore
farce, farse
farci, farcy, farsi
fare see fair
farer, farrier
farina, farine, farinha,
farm, form, forme, formee, forum
faro, farrow, furrow, pharoah
    see also Faerose
faros see Faerose
farrier see farer
farrow see faro
farse see farce
farsi see farci
farther, further see also father
fasces see faces
fascet see facet
fascial see facial
fassaite see facet
fassette see facet
fastuous, fatuous
fat, phat
fate see fait
fated, feted, fetid
father, fother see also farther
fattish see faddish
fatuous see fastuous
faucal, focal, phocal
fauces see faces
faucet, fossate, fossette see also
    facet
faults see false
faun, fawn
faunal, faunule
favose, favus
fawn see faun
fay, fei, fey

70

fays see face
faze see face
fazes see faces
feal, feel, feil, fjall, fjeld see
    also field
fear, feer, FERE, fiar
feat, feet, fete, fiat see also fait
feaze, fees, feeze
febrile, fibril
feces see faces
feel see feal
feels, fills, fils
feer see fear
fees see feaze
feet see feat
feeze see feaze
fei see fay
feign see fain
feil see feal
feint see faint
feirie see faerie
felicitate see facilitate
fella see fallow
fellah see fallow
fellen, felon
feller see fallow
felloe see fallow
fellow see fallow
felly see fallow
felon see fellen
fen, fin, Finn
fenestral, fenestrule
fenny, finny
feod, feud
feoff, fief see also fife
FERE see fear
FERIA
ferm, firm see also farm
FERMENT, foment
fermentation, fomentation
fermiere, firmer
fern, firn
ferrate, ferret, ferrite
ferrule, ferula, ferule
ferry see faerie
fers, firs, furs, furze
ferula see ferrub
ferule see ferrule
fervent, fervid

71

fete see feat and fait
feted see fated
fetial see facial
fetid see fated
fetish see faddish
fetor, fetter
feu, few, fou, phew
feuar, fewer
feud see feod
feudal, footle, futile
few see feu
fewer see feuar
fey see fay
feys see face
fez see face
fiancé, fiancée, finance
fiar see fear
fiat see fait and feat
fibber, fiber
fibril see febrile
fibrin, fibroin
fibrose, fibrous
fictitious see factitial
fie, phi
fief, feoff
field, filled see also feal
fife, five see also feoff
fight, fite
fike, fyke
fil, fill
filar, filer, phylar
filariid, filarioid
file, phial, phile, phyle see
    also fail and fil
filer see filar
filet, fillet
fili, filly
fill see fil
filled see field
fillet see filet
fillip, Philip (Phillip)
fillipeen, Philippine
fills see feels
filly see fili
fils see feels
filter, philter (philtre)
fin see fen
final, finale
finance see fiancé
financier, financière
find, fined

finis, finish, Finnish
Finn see fen
Finnic, finnock
Finnish see finis
finnock see Finnic
finny see fenny
fiord, ford/Ford, fyrd
fir, fur, furr
firm see form
firmer see fermiere
firn see fern
firry, furry
firs see fers
firth/Firth, furth/Furth
fishor, fissure
fishery, fissury
fissure see fisher
fissury see fishery
fite see fight
five see fife
fixer, fixture, fixure
fizz, phiz
fjall see feal
fjeld see feal
flac, flack, flak
flair, flare
flak see flac
flam, flamb, flambé, flame, fleam,
    fleme, phlegm, phleum, phloem
    see also flume
flammable, inflammable, nonflammable,
    non-inflammable
flare see flair
flaunt, flout
flavin, flavine
flay, fley
flea, flee
fleam see flam
flèche, flesh see also fleech
flecks, flex, flicks
flee see flea
fleech, fletch, flitch see also flèche
fleme see flam
flesh see fleche
fletch see fleech
fleuret, fleurette
flew, flu, flue
flews, flues
flex see flecks
fley see flay
flic, flick

73

flicks see flecks
flight, flite, flyte
flitch see fleech
flite see flight
fliting, flyting
floc, flock see also flac
flocks, phlox
floe, flow
flor, flour, flower
floral, florid
florin, fluorene, fluorine
flour see flor
flout see flaunt
flow see floe
flower see flor
flu see flew
flue see flew
flues see flews
flume, phlegm, phleum, phloem
    see also flam
fluorene see florin
fluorine see florin
flyboy, fly-boy
flyte see flight
flyting see fliting
foaled, fold
focal see faucal
fogey, foggy
fold see foaled
folder, foulder
FOLIATE, foliet
foment see ferment
fomentation see fermentation
fon, fond
fondu, fondue
fontanel, fontinol
foot, phut
footle see feudal
for see far
forbear, forebear
forceful, forcible
ford/Ford see fiord
fore, four see also far and fair
forebear see forbear
forego, forgo
foregone, forgone
forestal, forestall
forewarn, forwarn, forworn
foreword, forward, froward

74

forgo see forego
forgone see foregone
form see farm
formal, formol, formyl
formalize, formolize
formally, formerly
forme, see farm
formée see farm
formerly see formally
formol see formal
formolize see formalize
formulate, formylate
formyl see formal
formylate see formulate
forte, FORTE, forty
forth, fourth
fortin, fourteen
forty see fort
forum see farm
forward see foreword
forwarn see forewarn
forworn see forewarn
fossa, fosse
fossate see faucet
fosse see fossa
fossette see faucet
fother see father
fou see feu
fought, phot
foul, fowl
foulder, see folder
fouler, fowler
four see fore
FOURCHETTE
fourteen see fortin
fourth see forth
fowl see foul
fowler see fouler
fractur, fracture, fraktur
frae, fray, Frey, fry
fraise, frays, fraze, phrase see
    also frees
fraktur see fractur
franc, frank/Frank
Frances, Francis
frangipane, frangipani
frank/Frank see franc
frap, FRAPPE
frate, freight, freit, fright

75

frater, freighter
fraud, Freud
fray see frae
frays see fraise
fraze see fraise
frazil, frazzle
frees, freeze, frieze see also fraise
freight see frate
freighter see frater
freit see frate
FREQUENT
Freud see fraud
Frey see frae
friable, fryable
friar, fryer
frieze see frees
fright see frate
fro, froe
froes (frows), froze
froward see foreword
froze see froes
fry see frae
fryable see friable
fryer see friar
fucose, fucus
fug, fugue
fugal, fugle
fugue see fug
fun, fund
funeral, funereal
fungous, fungus
fur see fir
furfural, furfuryl
furioso, furious
furnace, furnish
furor, furore
furr see fir
furrow see faro
furry see firry
furs see fers
furth/Furth see firth/Firth
further see farther
furze see fers
fusel, fusil
futile see feudal
fyke see fike
fyrd see fiord

g, gee, ghee, gie
Gabar, gabber
gabby, gabi, gaby
gabelle, gable
gabi see gabby
gable see gabelle
Gabon, gaboon
gaby see gabby
gae, gay, gey
Gael, gail, gale see also gaol
Gaelic, Gallic
gaff, gaffe
gaffer, goffer, golfer see also gofer
gage, gauge
gail see Gael
gaily, galea, galei see also galley
gain, gaine, gane
gainer, gainor
gair, gare
gait, gate
gaiter, gator
gala, galah, Galla
galant, galante, GALLANT
galatea, galati
Galatian, Galician, Gelasian,
    gelation
galax, galaxy
gale see Gael
galea see gaily
galei see gaily
galena, gallina
galère, galerie, gallery
galet, galette, gallet
Galician see Galatian
galjoen, gallein, galleon, gallon,
    galloon
gall, Gaul
Galla see gala
GALLANT see galant
galleass, gallows, gallus
gallein see galjoen
galleon see galjoen
gallery see galère
gallet see galet
galley, Galli, gally see also gaily
gallina see galena
Gallic see Gaelic

gallin see galjoen
gallon see galjoen
galloon see galjoen
gallop, gallup/Gallup, galop
galloping, galopin
gallows see galleass
gallup/Gallup see gallop
gallus see galleass
gally see galley
galop see gallop
galopin see galloping
galt, gault
galway/Galway, galways
galore, glore, GLOWER
gam, gamme
gambel, gamble, gambol
gambet, gambette, gambit
gamble see gambel
gambol see gambel
gamie, gamy
gamin, gamine
gamme see gam
gammer, grammar, grammer
gamy see gamie
gane see gain
gang, gangue
gangling, ganglion
gangue see gang
gantlet, gauntlet
gaol, geal, gel, jaal, jail, jell
    see also Gael
gaper, gapper
gar, gaur
garbill, garble, garboil
garden, garten
gardener, jardiniere
gardez, guardee
gare see gair
gargle, gargoyle
garnet, garnett
garret, garrot, garrote
garrulous, garrulus
garry, Garrya, gary/Gary
garten see garden
garter, goiter, guarder
garvey, garvie
gary/Gary see garry
gassed, gast, ghast
gasthaus, guesthouse

gat, get, ghat, got
gata, gatha
gate see gait
gateward, gatewards
gatha see gata
Gathic, gothic/Gothic
gator see gaiter
gau, gaw
gauche, gosh
gaud, god/God
gauffre, gaufre
gauge see gage
Gaul see gall
gault see galt
gaum, goum, gum
gauntlet see gantlet
gaur see gar
gauss, gauze
gauzy, gawsie
gaw see gau
gawk, gowk
gawsie see gauzy
gay see gae
gazelle, ghazel
gazet, gazette
geal see gaol
gean, gene/Gene, jean/Jean, jeans
    see also genes
gear, ger
gee see g
geechee, geisha
gel see gaol
Gelasian see Galatian
gelation see Galatian
geld, gelt
gem, gym, jem, jim/Jim
gemoc, gymoc
gene/Gene see gean
genes, jeans see also gean
genial, guignol/Guignol
genic, gynic
genie, ginney, ginny, jenny, jinny
genius, genus
gens, gents
gent, Ghent
genteel, gentile/Gentile, gentle
gentilesse, gentleness
gentle see genteel
gentleness see gentilesse

gents _see_ gens
genus _see_ genius
geophilous, geophilus
ger _see_ gear
gerkin, gherkin
german/German, germane, germen
germander, gerrymander
germane _see_ german/German
germen _see_ german/German
gerrymander _see_ germander
gest, geste, jest
gesture, jester
get _see_ gat
gey _see_ gae
geyser, guiser
Ghandi, Gondi
ghast _see_ gassed
ghat (ghaut) _see_ gat
ghazel _see_ gazelle
ghee _see_ g
Ghent _see_ gent
gherkin _see_ gerkin
ghol, ghoul, goal, Goel, gool, gule
ghoulie, goalie
ghouls, gules
giaour, GYRE
gib, guib, jib
gibbous, gibbus, gibus
gibe, jibe
gibus _see_ gibbous
gie _see_ g
gig, gigue, jig
gild, gilled, guild
gilder, guilder
gilgai, gilguy
GILL, jill _see_ _also_ jeel
gilled _see_ gild
GILLIE, gilly
gilt, guilt
gimbal, gimble, gimel, gimmal, gymel
gimp, guimpe
gin _see_ djin
ginney _see_ genie
ginny _see_ genie
gip, gyp
gips, gyps
girl, gurl
girlie, gurly
gist, jist

GLACE, glass
glacier, glazer, glazier
gladden, gladdon
gladdy, glady
glair, glare, glaur
glairy, glary
glands, glans
glare see glair
glary see glairy
glass see GLACE
glassie, glassy
glaucous, glaucus
glaur see glair
glazer see glacier
glazier see glacier
gleamer, glimmer
glede, gleed
glent, glint
gleyde, glide
gliff, glyph
glimmer see gleamer
glint see glent
gloam, glom, gloom, glum, glume
global, globule
globulin, Gobelin, goblin
glom see gloam
gloom see gloam
glore see galore
glower see galore
glows, gloze
glum see gloam
glume see gloam
gluten, glutton
glycerol, glyceryl
glycin, glycine
glyph see gliff
gnap, knap, nap, nappe
gnat, nat, natte
gnaw, nao, naw
gnawer, knaur
gnaws, naos
gneiss, NICE
gnib, nib
gnome, no'm, nome/Nome
gnu, knew, new, nu
go, goa
goal see ghol
goala, gola, golah
goalie see ghoulie

goat, gote
gob, gobbe
Gobelin see globulin
gobi/Gobi, GOBY
goblin see globulin
GOBY see gobi/Gobi
god/God see gaud
Goel see ghol
goer, gore
gofer, gopher see also gaffer
Gogol, google, googol
goiter see garter
gola see goala
golah see goala
golden cress, golden crest
golfer see gaffer
Gondi see Ghandi
goodyear/Goodyear, goodyera
google see Gogol
googol see Gogol
gool see ghol
gopher see gofer
Gordian, guardian
gore see goer
gored, gourd, gourde
gorilla, guerilla
gospel, gossypol
gosh see gauche
gossypol see gospel
got see gat
gote see goat
gothic/Gothic see Gathic
goum see gaum
gourd see gored
gourde see gored
GOUT, goutte, gouty, gut, guttée,
    gutty see also guti
gowk see gawk
gracioso, gracious
gradation, graduation
grade, grayed
grader, grater, greater
GRADUATE
graduation see gradation
graft, graphed
graham/Graham, gram, grame, gramme
graisse, grass, grays, graze
gram see graham/Graham
grame see graham/Graham

grammar _see_ gammer
gramme _see_ graham/Graham
grammer _see_ gammer
granat, granite
grand, grande, grandee
grander, grandeur
granite _see_ granat
grantee, granthi
granter, grantor
granthi _see_ grantee
grantor _see_ granter
GRANULATE
graphed _see_ graft
grass _see_ graisse
grassie, grassy
grate, great
grater _see_ grader
gratin, gratten
GRAVE _see also_ greave
gray, grès
grayed _see_ grade
grays _see_ graisse
graze _see_ graisse
grazer, grazier
grease, Greece _see also_ gree
great _see_ grate
greater _see_ grader
greave, grieve _see also_ grave
greaves, grieves
gree, gris
Greece _see_ grease
gregal, gregale
greige, griege
grenadin, grenadine
Grendal, Grendel, grindle
grès _see_ gray
grew, grue, guru
griege _see_ greige
grievance, grievants
grieve _see_ greave
grieves _see_ greaves
griff, griffe
griffin/Griffin, griffon
grill, grille
grim, Grimm, grimme
grindle _see_ Grendal
grip, gripe, grippe
gris _see_ gree _and_ grease
grisly, gristly, grizzly

grison, grissen
gristly see grisly
grizzly see grisly
groan, groin, grown
groat, Grote
grocer, groser, grosser
groin see groan
groom, grume
gros, grow, gross
groser see grocer
gross see gros
grosser see grocer
Grote see groat
ground seal, groundsel
grouse, grouze
GROUSER
grouze see grouse
grow see gros
grown see groan
grue see grew
grume see groom
grus, gruss
guarantee, guaranty
guardee see gardez
guarder see garter
guardian see Gordian
Guarea, guarri
guddle, guttle
guerdon, gueridon
guerilla see gorilla
guernsey/Guernsey, jersey/Jersey
guess, guessed, guest
guesthouse see gasthaus
guib see gib
guide, guyed
guignol/Guignol see genial
guild see gild
guilder see gilder
guile, gyle
guilt see gilt
guimpe see gimp
guise, guys
guiser see geyser
gul, gull
gule see ghol
gules see ghouls
gull see gul
gum see gaum
gundi, gundy, gunny

gurl see girl
gurly see girlie
guru see grew
gut see GOUT
guttee see GOUT
gutty see GOUT
guti, guttie, gutty see also GOUT
guttle see guddle
gutty see Guti
guyed see guide
guys see guise
gyle see guile
gym see gem
gymel see gimbal
gymoc see gemoc
gynic see genic
gyp see gip
gyps see gips
GYRE see giaour
gyve, jive

H

ha, hah, HAUGH, haw see also HAUGH
    under separate listing
haar, hair, hare, harr
hachure, hasher
hackie, hacky
HADE, hades/Hades, hati
hae, hay, HEIGH, hey, high see also
    HEIGH under separate listing
haet, hait, hate, see also height
haff, half, halve, have
hag, Hague
haggy, hagi
Hague see hag
hah see ha
hahs, has, haws, hawse, hoss
haik, hake, hike
haiku, hokku
hail, hale, hell see also heal
hailer, haler
hair see haar
hary, harry/Harry
hait see haet
hake see haik
halcyon/Halcyon see alcyon
hale see hail
haler see hailer

85

half see haff
halide, halite
hall, haul, holl
hallo, hallow, halo, hello
halo see aloe and hallo
hals, halse, halts see also hahs
halve see haff
hameil, hamel
hammock, hummock
Han, hand
hance, hants, haunts, hence see also
    hence under separate listing
hand see Han
Handel, handle, hantle
handmade, handmaid
handsel, Hansel
handsome, hansom
hangar, hanger
hankle, hankul
Hansel see handsel
hansom see handsome
hantle see Handel
hants see hance
haply, happily
haras, harass, harras
hardie, hardy, hearty
hare see haar
harem, harum
harl, harle see also herl
harmonica see armonica
harr see haar
harras see haras
harry/Harry see hairy
hart, heart
harum see harem
has see hahs
hasher see hachure
haste, heist see also heist under
    separate listing
hate see haet
hati see HADE
HAUGH, hoc, hock, hok see also ha
haul see hall
haunts see hance
have see haff
haw see ha
hawkeye, hawkie, hawky
haws see hahs
hawse see hahs

86

hay see hae
hayrack, hayrick
hays, haze, heys
hazel/Hazel, hazle
headward, headword
heal, heel, he'll, hill see also hail
heald, healed
healer, heeler
heals, heels, hills
hear, heer, here
heard, herd
hearse, hers see also hoarse
heart see hart
heartburn, heartburning
hearty see hardie
heaume, holm, home
hech, heck
hectare, hector/Hector
HEDER, heeder
heel see heal
heeler see healer
heels see heals
heer see hear
heeze, he's
HEIGH, hi, hie, high see also hae
height, hight, hyte see also haet
heimin, hymen
heir see aer
heist, hoist see also haste
hell see hail
he'll see heal
heller, hellier
hello see hallo
helpmate, helpmeet
hem, heme, him, hymn
hemp, himp
hen, hin
hence, hints see also hance
hent, hint
her, herr
herd see heard
here see hear
heredity, heritage
herein, heroin, heroine, heron,
    herring
heritage see heredity
herl, hurl see also harl
hern, Herne
heroin see herein

87

heroine see herein
heron see herein
herr see her
herring see herein
hers see hearse
he's see heeze
heterogeneous, heterogenous,
     heterogynous
heteronomous,   heteronymous
hew, hue, Hugh
hewed, hued
hewer, hure
hey see hae
heys see hays
hi see HEIGH
hide, hied, hyde/Hyde
hie see HEIGH
hied see hide
high see hae and HEIGH
higher, hire
hight see height
hike see haik
hill see heal
hills see heals
him see hem
himp see hemp
hin see hen
HINDER
hint see hent
hints see hence
hip, hype
Hippocratic, hypercritical, hypocritical
hire see higher
his, hiss
hissed, hist
historical, hysterical
ho, hoe, hoh
hoar, hore, whore
hoard, horde, whored
hoarse, horse see also hearse
hoary, horry, whory
hoast, host
hobo, jobo
hoc see HAUGH
hock see HAUGH
hocks, hox see also HAUGH
hoe see ho
hoes, hose
hoh see ho
hoise, hoist see also heist

hok see HAUGH
hoke, howk
hokku see haiku
hokum, jocum
hole, whole
holey, holi, holly, holy, wholly
holl see hall
hollo, hollow see also hallo
holly see holey
holm see heaume
holy see holey
hombre, ombre, umber, umbre
home see heaume
homogeneous, homogenous, homogonous
honor, oner
hoop, whoop
hootch, hutch
hoping, hopping
hora, Horae
horde see hoard
hore see hoar
horror, whorer
horry see hoary
hors d'ouevres, orders
horse see hoarse
hose see hoes
hoss see hahs
host see hoast
hostal, hostel, hostile
hosteler, hostler, hustler
hostile see hostal,
hostler see hustler, hosteler
hostile see hostal
hostler see hosteler
hour see aar
houri, ourie
hours, ours
housel, ouzel
how, howe/Howe
howel, howell/Howell, howl
howk see hoke
howl see howel
hox see hocks
hue see hew
hued see hewed
Hugh see hew
human, humane, humin
humanism, humanitarianism, humism
humanist, humanistic, humanitarian

humanitarianism see humanism
humble, hummel, umbel
humbly, humlie
humeral, humoral
humerus, humorous
humin see human
humism see humanism
humlie see humbly
hummel see humble
hummock see hammock
humoral see humeral
humorous see humerus
hurdle, hurtle
hure see hewer
hurl see herl
hurri, hurry
hurtle see hurdle
hustler see hosteler
hutch and hootch
hyde/Hyde see hide
hydra/Hydra, hydria
hydras, hydrase
hydrocephalous, hydrocephalus
hyena, hyenia
hymen see heimin
hymn see hem
hype see hip
hypercritical see Hippocratic
hyperin, Hyperion, hyperon
hypertensin, hypertension
hypocritical see Hippocratic
hypogenous, hypogynous
hypotenuse, hypotonus
hysterical see historical
hyte see height

I

I see ai
icer see Aissor
Idaean see aition
idaein see aition
idea, ideal, itea/Itea see also idle
idealist, idyllist
ideate, idiot
idem, item
idiocy, idiosyncrasy
idiomatic, idiotic
idiosyncrasy see idiocy

idiot *see* ideate
idiotic *see* idiomatic
idle, idol, idyll *see also* idea
idyllist *see* idealist
ill *see* eel
I'll *see* aisle
illapse *see* elaps
illation *see* alation
illicit *see* elicit
illite *see* elide
illiterate *see* alliterate
illude *see* allude
illuminate *see* eliminate
illumine *see* alumen
illusion *see* allision
illusive *see* allusive
illusory *see* elusory
illuvial *see* alluvial
illuviate *see* alleviate
I'm *see* em
imaginary, menagerie
imbrue, imbue
imitate *see* amitate
immane *see* emane
immanence *see* eminence
immanent *see* emanant
immerge *see* emerge
immerse *see* amerce
immersed *see* emersed
immersion *see* emersion
immigrant *see* emigrant
immigration *see* emigration
imminence *see* eminence
imminent *see* emanant
immit *see* emit
immolate *see* emulate
immolation *see* emulation
immoral *see* amoral
immortal, immortelle
immunity, impunity
IMPACT
impair, impar
impassable, impassible
impatience, impatiens
imperial *see* empyreal
impetuous, impetus
implacement *see* emplacement
implastic *see* emplastic
IMPORT

91

imposter, imposture
impracticable, impractical
IMPRESS see empress
impressed, IMPREST
IMPRINT
improbability, improbity
impugn, impunity see also immunity
in see en
inadmissible, imamissible
inapt, inept, unapt
INCARNATE
in case see encase
INCENSE, insense
incidence, incidents
incident, incitant, insident
incidents see incidence
incipient, incipit, insipid
incision, insition
incitant see incident
incite, insight
inclose see enclose
INCORPORATE
INCREASE
incubuous, incubus
Ind see en
indemnitee, indemnity
indentation, indention
independence, independency
indian/Indian, Indiana, indienne/
    Indienne
indict, indite
indienne/Indienne see indian/Indian
indiscreet, indiscrete
indite see indict
individual see dividual
individualization, individuation
indoor, indore
indoors see endorse
indore see indoor
indorse see endorse
industrial, industrious
ineffective, ineffectual
inept see inapt
inequable, inequal
inequality, inequity
infans, infant, infanta, infante,
    infants
infect, infest
infectious, infestious, infestuous

92

infest see infect
infestious see infectious
infestuous see infectious
infirm, inform
INFIX
inflammable see flammable
inflect, inflict
influence, influents, influenza
inform see infirm
INFURIATE
ingenious see disingenuous
ingenuous see disingenuous
ingredience, ingredients
inhale, inhell
inhuman, inhumane
INITIATE
INLAY
innate see enate
inn see en
inner see enter
innervate see enervate
innocence, innocency, innocents
innumerable see enumerable
insense see INCENSE
insensible, insensitive
INSERT
insident see incident
insight see incite
insigne see ensign
insipid see incipient
insition see incision
insolation, insulation
installation, instillation
instance, instants
instillation see installation
insulation see insolation
INSULT
insure see ensure
intendance, intendence
intendiment, intendment
intense, intents
intension, intention
intents see intense
inter see enter
INTERCEPT
INTERCHANGE
intercoastal, intercostal
INTERCROSS
interdental, interdentil

INTERDICT
interess, interest
INTERMEDIATE
intermural, intramural
INTERN, internee, in-turn
interosseous, interosseus
interval, intervale
intervein, intervene
intervert, introvert
INTIMATE
in-turn see INTERN
intramural see intermural
intrant see entrant
INTRICATE
intrigant, intrigante
INTRIGUE
introvert see intervert
invade, inveighed
INVALID
inveighed see invade
INVERT
inverter, invertor
invest, vest
invious see envious
INVOLUTE
irascible see erasable
Irena, irene/Irene
iris/Iris, Irish
irk see erk
iron see arn
irrelevant, irreverent
irremeable, irremediable
irrepairable, irreparable
irreverent see irrelevant
irrigate, irrogate
irrupt see erupt
irruption see eruption
irruptive see eruptive
isle see aisle
islet see eyelet
isotac, isotach
Israel see Azrael
itea/Itea see idea
item see idem
its, it's, 'tis
Iyar see ear

J

j, jay
jaal see gaol
jacal, jackal
jacinth, jacinthe
jack/Jack, jauk, jock
jackal see jacal
Jacobian, Jacobin
jactation, jactitation
jaculate see ejaculate
jaeger, jager, jagger, jagir, jaguar
    see also chaguar
jail see gaol
jalap, jalopy
jalousie, jealousy
jam, jamb
jambeau, jambo, jumbo see also
    jambeaux
jambeaux, jambos see also jambeau
jambo see jambeau
jambos see jambeaux
jardiniere see gardener
jargon, jargoon
jarl, jarool
jasmine, jasmone
jasus, Jesus
jauk see jack/Jack
jaunce, jaunts, jounce
JAUNTY
jay see j
jealous, jealouse, zealous see also
    jalousie
jean/Jean see gean
jeel, jill/Jill see also GILL
jell see gaol
jem see gem
jemmies, jimmies
jemmy, jimmy
jen see djin
jenny see genie
jersey/Jersey see guernsey/Guernsey
jes, jess/Jess, jesse/Jesse see
    also gest
jest see gest
jester see gesture
Jesus see jasus
jeté, jetty
jeu, Jew

jewel, joule, jural, jurel, xurel
jewelry, jewels, jewry, jury
jib see gib
jibe see gibe
jig see gig
jill/Jill see jeel and GILL
jim/Jim see gem
jimmies see jemmies
jimmy see jemmy
jin see djin
jing see ching
jingal, jingle
jinks, jinx, jynx
jinn see djin
jinny see genie
jinx see jinks
jist see gist
jive see gyve
jo/Jo see CHOU
JOB
jobo see hobo
jock see jack/Jack
jocum see hokum
joe/Joe see CHOU
jointer, jointure
jokul, yokel
jook, juke
jorram, jorum
joule see jewel
jounce see jaunce
Judah, Judas, Jude
judicial, judicious
juggler, Juglar, jugular
juju, jujube
juke see jook
julep, tulip
julian/Julian, julienne/Julienne
Juliet, Juliett
jumbo see jambeau
Juneau, Juno
jungli, jungly
Juno see Juneau
jural see jewel
jurel see jewel
jury see jewelry
jus, just
justicer, justiciar
Juvenal, juvenile
jynx see jinks

K

k see cay
kaama see caama
kabbalah see Cabala
kaddish see caddis
kae see cay
Kaffir see kafir
kale, kell
Kama see caama
kame see came
kamerad see comrade
Kannada see Canada
Kant see cant
kantar see canter
kapelle see capella
kaph, kef
kaput see capot
karakul see caracal
karat see carat
karate see carat
karbi see corbie
karpas see carpus
karrusel see carousal
kat see cat
kate see cate
katel see caddle
kauri see corrie
kay see cay
kayak, kyack
kea see cay
kedge see cadge
keek, kick
keel, kiel, kill, kiln see also keen
keen, ken, kiln, kin see also keel
keest, kissed, kist
keet, kit
kef see kaph
kein, kind, kine
kell see kale
kelpie, kelpy
ken see keen
kermes, kermis
kern see curn
kernel see colonel
kerosene see characin
kerria, kerrie, kerris, kyrie
     see also carey and corrie
kerril, keryl
kerris see kerria

keryl see kerril
ketch see catch
ketol, kettle, ketyl
Kew see coo
key see cay
keys, quiyas see also cay
khan see can
kibbutz, kibitz, kibosh
kick see keek
kiddish, kiddush
kiel see keel
kiln see keen and keel
kilo see Chilo
kin see keen
kind see dein
kindal, kindle
KINDER
kindle see kindal
kine see kein
kinesthetic, kinetic
kirtle see curdle
kirve see curve
kissar, kisser
kissed see keest
kisser see kissar
kist see keest
kit see keet
kite, kyte
kith, kithe
kittel, kittle, kittul
Kiwai, kiwi
klan see clan
klatch see clash
kling see cling
klippe see clip
kloof see cloof
knack, nak
knacker, nacre
knag, nag
knap see gnap
knaur see gnawer
knave, naeve, naive, nave
knead, need
knee, nee see also nae
kneel, knell, neal, nell/Nell see
     also knell under separate listing
knees, neeze
knell, nail, nell/Nell see also kneel
knew see gnu

knicker, nicker
knight, night
knighted, nitid
knit, nit
knitch, niche
knob, nob
knobby, nobby
knock, nock
knocks, knox/Knox, nocks, nox
knoll, noll
knot, naught, not
knotty, naughty, noddy
know, no, Noah, Noh
knowed, node
knows, noes, no's, nose
knox/Knox see knocks
kohl see coal
Koine see coign
kolm see comb
Kongo see conga
kupper see cooper/Cooper
kor see car
Korea see chorea
korona see corona
kosher see cosher
kosin see cosine
kot see coat
kota see coda
koto see coteau
kraal see choral and crawl
krait, krit
kraken see cracking
kran see cran
krantz see crance
krasis see crasis
krater see crater
kraton see craton
kreis see chrysis
krill see creel
kris see crease
krit see krait
krona see corona
krone see corona
kroo see crew
kroon see croon
kru see crew
kuba see cuba/Cuba
Kuhlia, kula, Kulah
Kuki see cookie

kuku see cuckoo
kula see Kuhlia
kulah see Kuhlia
Kulaman see coolamon
Kulli see cully
kultur see couture
kulture see couture
kupper see cooper/Cooper
kurd see curd
Kure see CURE
kurrie see CURE
kurrajong see currawong
kurrol see curial
Kurukh see currack
kurus see crush
kuttar see cutter
kweek, quaich, quake, quick
kyack see kayak
Kyloe see Chilo
kyphosis, Kyphosus
Kyriale, kyrielle
kyte see kite
Kyurin see curine

L

l see el
laager, lager, logger see also
    laggar
label, labial, labile
labrus, labrys
lac, lack, lakh
lacerta, lacertae
laces, lacis
laches, latches
lacis see laces
lack see lac
lackey, lacquey
lacks, lax
lacquey see lackey
ladder, later, latter see also later
    under separate listing
lade, laid
laden, ladin see also lateen
laet, lat see also lait
lager see laager
laggar, lagger see also laager
laggard, laggered
lagger see laggar

100

laggered see laggard
laggin, lagging, leggings
lagopous, Lagopus
LAI, lay, lei, ley see also lea
laic, lake, lek
laid see lade
lain, laine, lane, layne
lair, layer, lehr see also LEAR
laird, layered
laisse, lays, laz, laze, leis
lait, late see also laet
lake see laic
lakh see lac
lam, lamb, LAME
lama, llama
lamb see lam
LAME see lam
land, lande
lane see lain
lang lay, langley
languor, langur
lap, Lapp
lapan, lapin
Lapp see lap
Lapps, laps, lapse
lard, lord/Lord see also laird
    and laud
lari, larry/Larry
larrigan, larrikin
larry/Larry see lari
larval, larvule
laser, lazar, lazer
last, latest
lat see laet
latches see laches
late see lait
lateen, laten, la tene, Latin,
    latten see also laden
later, latter, leder see also
    leader and ladder
latest see last
lath, lathe
Latin see lateen
latten see lateen
latter see ladder and later
lattice, let's, lettuce, let us
laud, lawd see also lard and laird
laurate, laureate
laurel, lauroyl, lauryl, loral, lorel
Laurus, loris

lauryl see laurel
lauter, lawter, loiter
laveer, laver
lawd see laud
lawn, loan, lone, loon, lown
lawter see lauter
lax see lacks
lay see lai
layer see lair
layered see laird
layne see lain
lays see laisse
laz see laisse
lazar see laser
laze see laisse
lazer see laser
lea, lee, li see also lai
leach, leech
LEAD, led
leader, lieder, liter, litter
leads, Leeds
leaf, leave, Leif, lief
leag, league
leak, leek
leal, lill
lean, lien
leaner, lienor
leant, lent, lint see also lend
LEAR, leer, lehr see also lair
leary, LEERY
lease, lees
leased, least, less, lest, loess
leaser, leisure
least see leased
leave see leaf
leaven, levin
lector, lecture
Lecythis, lecythus
led see LEAD
leder see later
lee see lea
leech see leach
Leeds see leads
leek see leak
leer see LEAR
leery see leary
lees see lease
legend, legion, lesion
leggings see laggin

legion see legend
legislator, legislature
legumen, legumin
lehr see lair
lei see lai
Leicester, leister
Leif see leaf
leis see laisse
leister see Leicester
leisure see leaser
lek see laïc
leks, lex
lem, limb, limn
Leman, lemon, liman, limen,
    limon/Limón
lemmer, lemur, lemure, limmer
lemon see Leman
lemur see lemmer
lemure see lemmer
lemures, lemurs
lend, linn see also leant
lends, lenis, lens, linis, linns
lengua, lingua, lingue
Lenin, linen, linin
lenis see lends
lens see lends
lent/Lent see leant
lenticel, lenticle
lentil, lintel
leprose, leprous
lerot, lerret
lesion see legend
less see leased
lessen, lesson
lessened, lessoned
lesser, lessor
lesson see lessen
lessoned see lessened
lessor see lesser
lest see leased
let, Lett, lit
lets, let's see also lattice
Lett see let
lettuce see lattice
let us see lattice
leu, lew, lieu, loo
Leucifer, lucifer/Lucifer
leud, lewd
levee, levy

103

lever, levier
levin see leaven
levy see levee
lew see leu
lewd see leud
lewis/Lewis, lues
lex see leks
ley see lai
li see lea
liable, libel
liar, lier, lyre
libel see liable
lice, lyse
licenser, licensure
lichen, liken, likin
lickerish, licorice, liquorice
lie, lye see also lai
lieder see leader
lief see leaf
lien see lean
lienor see leaner
lier see liar
lieu see leu
lightening, lightning
liken see lichen
likin see lichen
lill see leal
lily, Lyly
limacine, limousine
liman see Leman
limb see lem
limen see lemon
limey, limy
limmer see lemmer
limn see lem
limon/Limón see Leman
limousine see limacine
limy see limey
linage, LINEAGE
linch, lynch
lindane, linden
line, lion
LINEAGE see linage
lineal, linear
linen see Lenin
lingua see lengua
lingue see lengua
linin see Lenin
linis see lends

104

links, lynx
linn see lend
linns see lends
lint see leant
lintel see lentil
lion see line
liqueur, liquor
liquorice see lickerish
LIRA
lirk, lurk
lisa/Lisa, lyssa
lit see let
liter see leader
literal, littoral
literator, literature, litterateur
lithe, lythe
litter see leader
litterateur see literator
littoral see literal
LIVE
liver, livre
llama see lama
lo, low
load, lode, lowed
loan see lawn
loath, loathe, loth
local, locale
loch, Locke, lock, lough
lochs, locks, loughs, lox
lock see loch
locks see lochs
locus, locust
lode see load
loess see leased
log, loge
logger see laager
loggie, loggy, logy
loiter see lauter
lone see lawn
longue, lounge
loo see leu
loon, lune see also lawn
loons, lunes
loop, lope, loop, loupe
loose, lose, loss see also lewis/
    Lewis
looser, loser, losser
loosing, losing
loot, lute

lope see loop
loral see laurel
lord/Lord see lard
lore, LOWER
lorel see laurel
loris see Laurus
lorry, lory
lose see loose
loser see looser
losing see loosing
loss see loose
losser see looser
loth see loath
lough see loch
loughs see lochs
LOUK
lounge see longue
loup see loop
loupe see loop
louvar, louver, Louvre, lover
low see lo
lowed see load
LOWER see lore
lown see lawn
lox see lochs
lucern, lucerne/Lucerne
lucifer/Lucifer see Leucifer
Luciferian, luciferin
lues see lewis/Lewis
lumbar, lumber
lumen, lumine
lune see loon
lunes see loons
lupulin, lupuline
lur, lure
lurk see lirk
lute see loot
Lutheran, luthern
lux, luxe
lyceum, lycium
lye see lie
Lyly see lily
lynch see linch
lynx see links
lyre see liar
lyse see lice
lysin, lysine
lyssa see lisa/Lisa
lythe see lithe

M

m see em
ma, maw
ma'am, malm
maar, mar
macaroni, macaroon
mace, maize, maze
macer, maizer, maser, mazar, mazer,
    Mazur
mach/Mach, mock
mackle, macle
macrocosm, microcosm
madam, madame
madder, mador, mater, matter
made, maid
Madi, Mahdi
mador see madder
mae, may/May see also mai
maggot, magot
magisterial, magistral
magnate, magnet
magot see maggot
Mahdi see Madi
mai, my see also mae
maid see made
maidan, maiden
mail, male, mell see also maile
maile, Malay, mallee, melee, milieu
    see also mail
mailer, malar
main, Maine, mane, mesne
mains, manes
mair, mare, mayer, mayor
maize see mace
maizer see macer
makar, maker
malar see mailer
malate, mallet
Malay see maile
male see mail
malign, maline, milline
mall, maul, moll
mallee see maile
mallet see malate
mallow, mellow, meloe
malm see ma'am
maltase, maltese, maltose
mama or mamma or momma, mammer

mamba, mambo
mammary, memory
mammer _see_ mama
mana, manna
manage, manege, menage
mancipate _see_ emancipate
mancipation _see_ emancipation
mandlen, mandolin
mandrel, mandrill
mane _see_ main
manege _see_ manage
manes _see_ mains
mangel, mangle
maniac, manic, manioc
manila/Manila, manilla, manille
manioc _see_ maniac
manna _see_ mana
manner, manor
MANQUE, monkey
manteel, mantel, mantle
many, meiny
mar _see_ maar
marabou, marabout/Marabout
maraca, morocco/Morocco
Marasmius, marasmus
marc, mark/Mark, marque, marquee
marchant, merchant
mare _see_ mair
marginalia, marginella
Mari, marri/Marri, marry, mary/
      Mary, merry
mark/Mark _see_ marc
marker, markhor
marks, Marx
marli, marly
marlin, marline, merlin/Merlin
      see _also_ merlin/Merlin _under_
      separate listing
marly _see_ marli
maroon, marron
marque _see_ marc
marquess, marquis, marquise
marri/Marri _see_ Mari
marron _see_ maroon
marrow, Moro, morrow
marry _see_ mari
marshal, marshall/Marshall, martial
marsian, martian/Martian
mart, mort, morte

108

marten, martin/Martin
martial see marshal
martian/Martian see marsian
martin/Martin see marten
martinet, martineta, martinete
martyr, mortar
Marx see marks
Mary see mari
maser see macer
mask, masque
mass, mess
massage, message, messuage
massed, mast
masseur, masseuse, monsieur
massif, massive
mast see massed
mat, matte
mater see madder
material, materiel
matin, matine
matrass, matross, mattress
matte see mat
matter see madder
mattress see matrass
maud, mod
maul see mall
maun, maund
maundy, Monday
mauve, move
maw see ma
may see mae
may be, maybe
mayer see mair
mayor see mair
mazar see macer
maze see mace
mazer see macer
Mazur see macer
me, mi see also mae and mai
mead, Mede, meed
mealie, mealy
mean, mesne, mien
meandrine, meandering
meant, mint
mease, mise
meat, meet, mete
medal, meddle, metal, metol, mettle
meddler, medlar
Mede see mead

109

median, mediant, medium
medlar see meddler
meed see mead
meet see meat
meiny see many
melanose, melanous
melee see maile
Meles, melis
mell see mail
mellow see mallow
meloe see mallow
mem, mim
memory see mammary
men, min
menage see manage
menagerie see imaginary
menstruation see administration
menthanal, menthenal
meow, mew, moo, moue, mu
mer, mere, mir, murr, murre, myrrh
merchant see marchant
mere see mor
meridian, meridienne, Meridion
merl, merle, murl
merlin/Merlin, merlon see also marlin
merry see mari
mesne see main and mean
meson, messan
mess see mass
message see massage
messan see meson
messuage see massage
metal see medal
metanym, metonym
mete see meat
meteor, meter, métier
metol see medal
metonym see metanym
mettle see medal
mew see meow
mewl, mool, mule
mews, muse
mho, moa
mi see me
microcosm see macrocosm
micropterous, micropterus
midst, missed, mist
mien see mean
might, mite

migraine, migrans, migrant
mil, mill
milch, milk
milestone, millstone
milieu see maile
milk see milch
mill see mil
millenary, millenniary, millinery,
    millionaire
milline see malign
millinery see millenary
millionaire see millenary
millstone see milestone
mim see mem
min see men
mina, myna
minar, miner, minor, mynheer
mince, mints
mind, mine
miner see minar
minim, minimum, minium
minister, minster see also administer
ministration see administration
minium see minim
minks, minx
minor see minar
minster see minister
mint see meant
mints see mince
minuet, MINUTE
minx see minks
mir see mer
mise see mease
miser, mizar
misogamy, misogyny
missal, missile, mistle see also
    mistal
missed see midst
misses, Mrs.
missile see missal
mist see midst
mistal, mistelle see also missal
mite see might
mitraille, mitral
mizar see miser
moa see mho
moan, mown
moat, mote
mock see mach/Mach

111

mod see maud
modal, model, module, mottle
mode, mowed
model see modal
modeled, mottled
modest, modiste
modius, modus
module see modal
modus see modius
moer, mohair, mohar, mohr, mohur,
    moor, moore/Moore, mor, more/
    More, mower
mol, mole see also mold
mold, mould see also mol
molder, moulder
mole see mol
moll see mall
mollie/Mollie, molly/Molly
mondaine, mundane
Monday see maundy
monkey see MANQUE
monogeneous, monogenous, monogynous
monseigneur, monsignor see also
    masseur
monsieur see masseur
monsignor see monseigneur
moo see meow
mood, mooed
mool see mewl
moor see moer
moore/Moore see moer
moose, mouse, mousse
moot, mute
mor see moer
moral, morale, morral
morass, morris/Morris, morse/Morse
mordant, mordent
more/More see moer
morgan/Morgan, morgen
morn, MORNE, mourn
morning, mourning
Moro see marrow
morocco/Morocco see maraca
morral see moral
morris/Morris see morass
morrow see marrow
morse/Morse see morass
mort see mart
mortar see martyr

morte see mart
MOSEY, Mossi, mossie, mossy
mote see moat
motif, motive
mottle see modal
mottled see modeled
moue see meow
mould see mold
moulder see molder
mourn see morn
mourning see morning
mouse see moose
mousse see moose
moutan, mouton, mutton
move see mauve
MOW
mowed see mode
mower see moer
mown see moan
Mrs. see misses
mu see meow
mucous, mucus
mule see mewl
muleta, muletta
mun, mund
mundane see mondaine
murl see merl
murr see mer
murre see mer
musar, muser
muscat, musket
muscle, mussal, mussel, muzzle
muse see mews
muser see musar
muset, musette
music, muzhik
musket see muscat
mussal see muscle
mussed, must
mussel see muscle
must see mussed
mustard, mustered
mute see moot
mutton see moutan
mutual, mutuel
muzhik see music
muzzle see muscle
my see mai
myna see mina

mynheer see minar
myrrh see mer
mystic, mystique

N

n see en
nacelle, nasal, naselle
nacre see knacker
nae, nai, nay, nee, neigh see also
    knee
naeve see knave
nag see knag
nai see nae
nail see knell
naily, nelly/Nelly
nair/Nair, Nayar, nayaur, neigher
naissant, nascent
naive see knave
naggar, nagger
nak see knack
nambe, namby
nankeen, nankin, Nanking
nannie, nanny
nao see gnaw
naos see gnaws
nap see gnap
naphthol, naphthyl
nappe see gnap
nardic, Nordic
nasal see nacelle
nascent see naissant
naselle see nacelle
nat see gnat
natte see gnat
naught see knot
naughty see knotty
nautch, notch
naval, navel
nave see knave
navel see naval
navet, navette
navvy, navy
naw see gnaw
nay see nae
Nayer see nair/Nair
nayaur see nair/Nair
neal see kneel
neap, neep

near, neer
nectarous, necturus
nee see knee and nae
need see knead
neep see neap
neer see near
neeze see knees
neigh see nae
neigher see nair
neither, nether
nell see kneel and knell
nelly/Nelly see naily
nematic, pneumatic
nervose, nervous, nervus
nester, Nestor
nether see neither
new see gnu
Newcomb, newcome
newer, Nuer
New Licht, New Light, newlight
news, noose, nous
nib see gnib
NICE, niece see also gneiss
niche see knitch
nicker see knicker
nicks, nix
nidal, niddle
nidor, niter
niece see NICE
Niger, nigre
night see knight
nigre see Niger
nikau, Nikko
nil, nill
nimbose, nimbous
Nisei, nisi, nisse
nit see knit
niter see nidor
nitid see knighted
nix see nicks
no see know
Noah see know
nob see knob
nobby see knobby
Nobel, noble
nobles, noblesse
nock see knock
nocks see knocks
nocturn, nocturne

nodal, notal
noddy see knotty
node see knowed
nodulose, nodulus
noel/Noel, nowel
noes see knows
Noh see know
noisome, noisy
noll see knoll
no'm see gnome
Nome see gnome
nomen, numen
nominee, nominy
non, none, nun
nonce, nones, nuance
none see non
nones see nonce
nonflammable see flammable
non-inflammable see flammable
nonsked, nonskid
noose see news
Nordic see nardic
norman/Norman, Normand
no's see knows
nose see knows
not see knot
notal see nodal
notar, noter
notch see nautch
noter see notar
nous see news
nowel see noel/Noel
nox see knocks
nu see gnu
nuance see nonce
nucleolus, nucleus
Nuer see newer
nul, null
nulla, nullah
numen see nomen
nun see non

O

O see eau
oak, oke
oam see aum
oar, o'er, or, ore see also aar
    and aer

obdurate, obturate
obeah, obey, obi see also abe
obedience see abeyance
obeisance see abeyance
obese, obeys
obey see obeah
obeys see obese
obi see obeah
OBJECT
obol, obole
obturate see obdurate
occasion see Acacian
octanal, octanol
octroi, octroy
od, odd
odder, otter
ode, owed
Oder, odor
odeum, odium
odor see Oder
oe see eau
o'er see oar
of, off, oft
offal see awful
OFFENSE
oft see of
oh see eau
ohm see aum
ohms see alms
oil see ahl
oke see oak
oleo, olio
olm see aum
om see aum
Oman, omen
ombre see hombre
omission see amission
omit see emit
on see aune
once, wants, wanze see also wanes
ondine, undine
one, wan, wand, won
oner see honor
on to, onto
opah, ope
oppose see appose
opposite see apposite
opposition see apposition
oppressed see appressed

117

oppression see appression
or see aar
oracle see auricle
oral see aural
orbital, orbitale
orbiter see arbiter
orc see arc
orchestral, orchestrelle
orchis/Orchis see arcus
order see arder
orders see hors d'ouevres
ordinance, ordnance, ordonnance
ordure see arder
ORE see aar
Oregon see argon
Orel see aural
orf, orfe
organ see argon
organal, organelle
orgue see argue
oriel see aural
origan see argon
Origen see argon
origin see argon
oriole see aural
orogen see argon
orris see arras/Arras
ort see art
oscillate, osculate
osmesis, osmosis
osmose, osmous
osmosis see osmesis
osmous see osmose
osone, ozone
ostracean, Ostracion
Ostrea, Ostrya
Otis, Otus
ottava, Ottawa
otter see odder
otto/Otto see auetó
Otus see Otis
ought see aught and see naught
    under knot
our see aar
ourie see houri
ours see hours
ouse see ewes
outcast, outcaste
outler, outlier

outray, outré, out-tray
ouvert, overt
ouzel see housel
overchute, overshoot
overdo, overdue
overlade, overlaid
OVERPASS
OVERRUN
overseas, oversees
oversew, oversow
overshoot see overchute
overt see ouvert
ow see eau
owe see eau
owed see ode
owl see aoul
own see aune
owning see awning
oxen see auxin
oxhide, oxide
ozone see osone

P

p, pea, pee
pa, pah, pas, paw
pace, pays, pes
paced, paste
packed, pact
packs, pacts, pax see also pocks
pact see packed
pacts see packs
padder, pater, patter
paddle, patel
paddy, pattée, patty, paty
paean, paeon, peon see also pagne
      and pain and pean
pagne, pan/Pan, panne, paon see also
      paean and pain and pean
pah see pa
pail, pal, pale
paillette, palate, palet, palette,
      pallet, pallette
paillon, pylon
pain, pane see also pagne and paean
      and pean
paint, pant
paints, pants
pair, pare, pear, père

119

pairing, paring
pairle, parel, parrel see also pearl
paisano, paysanne
pal see pail
palace, palais, Pallas, palliasse,
    palouse, palus
palar, pallar, pallor
palate see paillette
pale see pail
palea, palely, pali, paly
palet see paillette
palette see paillette
pali see palea
pall, Paul, pawl
palla, pallah
pallar see palar
Pallas see palace
pallet see paillette
pallette see paillette
palliasse see palace
pallor see palar
palma, palmae
palmar, palmer/Palmer
palmette, palmetto
palmist, palmiste
palouse see palace
palpate, palpitate
palpation, palpitation
palpitate see palpate
palpitation see palpation
palus see palace
paly see palea
pamper, pampre
pan/Pan see pagne
PANACHE
pander, pandour
pandit, pundit
pandour see pander
pane see pain
panel, pannel
panne see pagne
pannel see panel
pannose, pannus
pant see paint
pantaleon, pantaloon
pants see paints
paon see pagne
papa, papaw
papagallo, papagayo

papaw see papa
papillon, papion
papoose, pappose, pappus
par, parr
parable, parabola
paragnathous, paragnathus
paragon, perigon
paralaxis, paralexia, parallax,
    paralysis
parameter, perimeter
paranoid, pyrenoid
paraphrase, periphrase
parasite, pericyte
pardhan, pardon
pardner, pardoner, partner
pare see pair
parel see pairle
parentalia, parentela
pareses, paresis
paring see paring
parish, perish
pariti, parity
park, parque, pork
parka, Parkia
parkin, parking
parlay, parley
parol, parole, payroll, prole, pyrrole
parotid, parroted
parque see park
parr see par
parrel see pairle
parroted see parotid
parry, peri, perry/Perry
parshall, partial
part, port, porte
parter, parterre
parti, party
partial see parshall
partner see pardner
party see parti
pas see pa
pascal/Pascal, paschal see also
    pascual
pase, pass, passé see also pa
pasquil see pascual
pass see pase
passable, passible
passage, paysage
passé see pase

passed, past see also paced
passel, pas seul
passible see passable
past see passed
paste see paced
pastel, pastille
Pasteur, pastor, pasture see also poster
pastiche, postiche
pastille see pastel
pastime, past-time
pastor see Pasteur
pastoral, pastorale, pastural
past-time see pastime
pastural see pastoral
pasture see Pasteur
pas seul see passel
PATE
patel see paddle
paten, patten, Patton see also PATENT
pater see padder
patience, patients
patrol, petrel, petrol
patron, patronne, patroon
pattée see paddy
patten see paten
patter see padder
Patton see paten
pattu, patu
patty see paddy
patu see pattu
paty see paddy
Paul see pall
paulin, Pauline
paup, pop
pauper, popper
pause, paws
paut, pot, pout
pavilion, pavillon
paw see pa
pawl see pall
Pawnee, pony
paws see pause
pax see packs and pocks
pay, pe
payroll see parol
pays see pace
paysage see passage
paysanne see paisano
pe see pay
pea see p
peace, peas, pease, peise, piece
peachy, pitchi, pitchy

peak, peek, PIQUE, piquet see also
    picket
peaking, peeping, Peking
peaky, piki
peal, peel, pill
pean, peen see also paean
pear see pair
pearl, perle, pirl, purl see also
    pairle
pearly, pirlie
peart, pert
peas see peace
pease see peace
peat, Pete
pecan, pekan, Pekin, Peking
pecari, peccary
peccancy, piquancy
peccant, piquant
peccary see pecari
peckle, pickel, pickle, picul, pikel
pecten, pectin
pectinal, pectineal
pectose, pectous, pectus
pedal, peddle, petal, pettle
pedicel, pedicle, pedocal
pediculous, pediculus
pedipalpous, pedipalpus
pedocal see pedicel
pee see p
peek see peak
peel see peal
peen see pean
peeping see peaking
peeps, Pepys
peepy, pipi, pippy
peer, pier
peeress, pierce/Pierce
peewee, pewee
peg, pegh
peise see peace
pekan see pecan
Pekin see pecan
Peking see peaking and pecan
pekoe, picot
pelisse, police, polis, polys
pen, pin
pencel, pencil, pensile
pend, penned, pind, pinned
pendant, pendent

pendill, pendle
penguin, pinguin
penitence, penitents
penna, pennae, penni, penny, pinna,
    pinnae, pinny
penned see pend
penner, pinner
pennon, pignon, pinion, piñon
penni see penna
penny see penna
pensile see pencel
peon see paean
people, pipal, pipil, pipple
peplis, peplos
Pepys see peeps
per, purr
perceive see apperceive
perceant, percent, precent, PRESENT
perception see apperception
père see pair
peregrina, peregrine
PERFECT, prefect
perficient, proficient
PERFUME
perfuse, profuse
perfusion, profusion
peri see parry
perichondral, perichondrial
pericyte see parasite
perigon see paragon
perimeter see parameter
periodic, periotic
periphrase see paraphrase
perish see parish
perle see pearl
PERMIT
pern, perne, pirn
perquisite, prerequisite
perry/Perry see parry
perse, purrs, purse
persecute, prosecute
persecutor, prosecutor
Persian, persienne
personal, personnel
PERSONATE
personnel see personal
perspicacity, perspicuity
pert see peart
pertain see appertain

pertinence, purtenance
pertinent *see* appurtenant
pervade, purveyed
PERVERT
pes *see* pace
petal *see* pedal
Pete *see* peat
petillant, petulant
petit, petite, petty
petrel *see* patrol
petrol *see* patrol
pettle *see* pedal
petty *see* petit
petulant *see* petillant
pew, piu, pugh
pewee *see* peewee
Phaëthon, phaeton
phare *see* fair
Pharoah *see* faro
Pharoahs *see* faerose
pharos/Pharos *see* Faerose
phase *see* face
phaser, phasor
phases *see* faces
phasis *see* faces
phasor *see* phaser
phat *see* fat
phenol, phenyl
phew *see* feu
phi *see* fie
phial *see* file
phile *see* file
Philip (Phillip) *see* fillip
Philippine *see* fillipeen
philter *see* filter
phiz *see* fizz
phlegm *see* flume *and* flam
phleum *see* flume *and* flam
phloem *see* flume *and* flam
phlox *see* flocks
phocal *see* faucal
phon, phone
phosphorous, phosphorus
phot *see* fought
photometeor, photometer
phototrophic, phototropic
phrase *see* fraise
phut *see* foot
phylar *see* filar
phyle *see* file

125

phylostomous, phylostomus
physic, physique see also physics
physics, physiology see also physic
physique see physic
physocarpous, physocarpus
pi, pie
PIA
pial, pile, pyal
PIANO
piat, piet
piatti, piety
pic, pick, pik
picarel, pickerel, picryl
picarii, pickery, picory
picaro, piquero
pick see pic
picked, Pict
pickel see pecile, peckle
pickerel see picarel
pickery see picarii
picket, piquet see also peak
pickle see peckle
picks, Picts, pix, pyx
picnic, pyknic
picory see picarii
picot see pekoe
picryl see picarel
Pict see picked
Picts see picks
picture, pitcher
picul see peckle
pidgin, pigeon
pie see pi
piece see peace
pier see peer
pierce/Pierce see peeress
pies, pize
piet see piat
piety see piatti
pigeon see pidgin
pignon see pennon
pik see pic
pike/Pike, pyke
pikel see peckle
piki see peaky
pilar, piler see also pillar
Pilate, pilot, piolet
pile see pial
pileous, pileus, pilose, pilus

126

piler see pilar
pileus see pileous
PILI
pill see peal
pillar, pillow see also pilar
pilose see pileous
pilot see Pilate
pilus see pileous
pimenta, pimento, pimiento
pin see pen
pinacol, pinnacle, pinochle
pincer, pincher
pincers, pinchers
pincher see pincer
pinchers see pincers
pind see pend
Pindar, pinder
pinquin see penguin
pinion see pennon
PINITE
pinna see penna
pinnace, pinnas
pinnacle see pinacol
pinnae see penna
pinnas see pinnace
pinned see pend
pinner see penner
pinny see penna
pinochle see pinacol
piñon see pennon
piolet see Pilate
pious, Pius
pipal see people
piperonal, piperonyl
pipi see peepy
pipil see people
pipple see people
piquancy see peccancy
piquant see peccant
pippy see peepy
PIQUE see peak
piquero see picaro
piquet see peak and picket
pirate, pyrite, pyrites, pyrrhite
pirl see pearl
pirlie see pearly
pirn see pern
pistil, pistol, pistole
pitcher see picture

pitchi see peachy
pitchy see peachy
piu see pew
Pius see pious
pix see picks
pixie, pyxie
pize see pies
placate, plicate
place, plaice
PLACER
plack, plaque
plaice see place
plaid, played, pleiad/Pleiad
plain, plane, plein
plainer, planar, planer, planner
plains, planes
plaint, plant
plaintiff, plaintive
planar see plainer
planchet, planchette
plane see plain
planer see plainer
planes see plains
planner see plainer
plant see plaint
plantar, planter see also plainer
plaque see plack
plastic, plastique
platan, platen
platanist, Platonist
platen see platan
Platonist see platanist
PLATY
played see plaid
plea, plié
pleas, please
pleiad/Pleiad see plaid
plein see plain
plene, plenty
plenteous, plentiful
plenty see plene
pleural, plural, plurel
plexor, plexure
plicate see placate
plié see plea
plough, plow
plouk, pluck
plum, plumb
plural see pleural/plurel see pleural

pneumatic see nematic
poa, poe/Poe, poh
pocks, pox see also packs
poddy, potty
poe/Poe see poa
poem, pome, pomme, proem
poesy, posy
poetic, poietic
poggy, pogy
pogrom, program, programme
pogy see poggy
poh see poa
poietic see poetic
point, pointe
poison, poisson/Poisson
pokey, poky
polar, poler
pole/Pole, poll
poleax, pollex
poler see polar
police see pelisse
poling, polling
polis see pelisse
POLISH
politeness, politesse
politic, politick
poll see pole/Pole
pollan, pollen
pollex see poleax
polling see poling
polydactylous, polydactylus
polypous, polypus
polys see pelisse
pomace, pumice
pome see poem
pomme see poem
pommel, pummel
pom-pom, pompon
pony see Pawnee
pood, poohed
poodle, puddle
poohed see pood
pooka, puka, pukka
pool, poule, pule
poor, puer, pure see also pore and puree
pop see paup
poplar, popular
popper see pauper
populace, populous, populus
popular see poplar
populous, populus see populace
populus see populace

porpoise, purpose see also prepose
pore, pour see also poor
pork see park
poros, porous
Porphyro, porphyra, porphyria,
    porphyry see also porphyrin
porphyrin, porphyrine see also Porphyro
porphyry see Porphyro
port see part
portato, potato
porte see part
portend, portent
porter, portiere
poser, poseur
posit, posset
poster, posture see also Pasteur
posterity, prosperity
postiche see pastiche
postulant, postulate
posture see poster
posy see poesy
pot see paut
potato see portato
potty see poddy
pouf, puff
poule see pool
pour see pore
pout see paut
pox see pocks and packs
practicable, practical
praecipe, precipice
praise, praiss, prase, prays, press,
    preys see also appraise
pratol, prattle, pretil
prau, prow
prawn, prone
pray, prey
PRAYER, preyer
prays see praise
precede, proceed
precedence, precedents, presidency,
    presidents
precedent, president
precedents see precedence
precent see perceant
precentor, presenter
préces, precess see also précis
precession, presession, procession
    see also precision
précieuse, precious
precipice see praecipe

130

précis, precis, precise see also
    préces
precisian, precision see also
    precession
PREDICATE
predominant, predominate
predominantly, predominately
predominate see predominant
predominately see predominantly
pree, prix
prefect see PERFECT
PREFIX, prix fixe
prefixation, prefixion
premier, premiere
premonition, premunition
PREPONDERATE
prepose, propose, purpose see
    also porpoise
preposition, prepossession,
    proposition
prerequisite see perquisite
presbyter, presbytére
prescribe, proscribe
presence, presents
PRESENT see perceant
presenter see precentor
presents see presence
presession see precession
presidency see precedence
president see precedent
presidents see precedence
press see praise
pressed, prest
presser, pressor, pressure
prest see pressed
prestidigitation, prestigiation
prestidigitator, prestigiator
prestigiation see prestidigitation
prestigiator see prestidigitator
pretil see pratol
pretty, prithee, purdy
prey see pray
preyer see PRAYER
preys see praise
price, pries, prise, prize
pride, pried
prier, prior
pries see price
PRIMER, primeur, primmer

prince, prints
princes, princess
principal, principle
prints see prince
prior see prier
prise see price
prithee see pretty
privacy, privity
private, privet
privity see privacy
prix see pree
prix fixe see prefix
prize see price
proceed see precede
PROCEEDS
procession see precession
procurer, procureur
PRODUCE
proem see poem
proestrous, proestrus
proficient see perficient
profit, prophet
profuse see perfuse
profusion see perfusion
program see pogrom
programme see pogrom
PROGRESS
PROJECT
PROLATE
prole see parol
prolong, prolonge
promiser, promisor, promissor
prone see prawn
propale, propel
propanal, propenyl
prophecy, prophesy
prophet see profit
propose see prepose
proposition see preposition
pros, prose
proscribe see prescribe
prose see pros
prosecute see persecute
prosecutor see persecutor
prosperity see posterity
prostate, prostrate
protean, protein
protégé, protégée
protein see protean

PROTEST
protogene, protogine
provenance, Provence, providence/
     Providence, province
Provencal, provincial
Provence see provenance
providence/Providence see provenance
province see provenance
provincial see Provencal
prow see prau
proximate see approximate
pruinous, Prunus
Prunella, prunelle
Prunus see pruinous
psalter, salter
psaltery, saltery
psammon, salmon
pshaw, shah, shaw/Shaw
psi, sie, sigh, sye
psis, sighs, size, syce
psittaceous see cetaceous
psychal see cycle
psychiatrist, psychoanalyst,
     psychologist see also physic
     and physics
psychosis, sycosis
psylla, Psyllia, scilla, Scylla
pteris, terrace
pterocarpous, pterocarpus
pteron, Tehran, terron see also
     terrain
ptisan, tisane
pubes, pubis
puddle see poodle
puer see poor
puerpera, purpura
puerperal, purpureal
puff see pouf
pugh see pew
puka see pooka
pukka see pooka
pul, pull
pule see pool
pull see pul
pumice see pomace
pummel see pommel
punctate, punctuate, punctulate
pundit see pandit
pungey, pungi

133

pupal, pupil
purdy see pretty
pure see poor
puree, purey, puri, purree
purl see pearl
purpose see porpoise and prepose
purpura see puerpera
purpureal see puerperal
purr see per
purree see puree
purrs see perse
purse see perse
purtenance see pertinence
purveyed see pervade
pus, puss
push, putsch
puss see pus
put, putt
putsch see push
putt see put
puttee, putty
PUTTER
putty see puttee
pyal see pial
pyke see pike
pyknic see picnic
pylon see paillon
pyorrhea, pyuria
pyrenoid see paranoid
pyric, pyrrhic/Pyrrhic
pyrite see pirate
pyrites see pirate
pyrrhic/Pyrrhic see pyric
pyrrhite see pirate
pyrrole see parol
pyuria see pyorrhea
pyx see picks
pyxie see pixie

Q

q see coo
qadi see caddie
qat see cat
qoph see cauf
qua, quay see also cay
quack see couac
quacksalver, quicksilver
quad, quod

134

quadrat, quadrate
quadrel see cuadrilla
quadrille see caudrilla
quaere, quare, quarry, queer, query
quaestor, questor, questeur
quaff see cauf
quai see cay
quaich see kweek
quail, quale, quell
quake see kweek
quale see quail
qualmish, quamash
quarantine, quarentene
quare see quaere
quarentene see quarantine
quark, quirk
quarl, quarrel
quarry see quaere
quarts, quartz
quay see cay and qua
quean, queen
queer see quaere
quell see quail
query see quaere
quester see quaestor
questeur see quaestor
questioner, questionnaire
queue see coo
quey see cay
quick see kweek
quicksilver see quacksalver
quidder, quitter, quittor
quiescence, quiescents
quiet, quite
quince, quintes, quints
quinine, quinone
quintal, quintile
quinte see cant
quintes see quince
quintile see quintal
quints see quince
quire see choir
quirk see quark
quis see cuisse
quite see quiet
quitter see quidder
quittor see quidder
quivery see cuivré
quiyas see keys
quiz see cuisse
quod see quad

quoin see coign
quote, quoth, quotha
qursh see currish

R

r see aar
Ra, rah
raad, rad
raan, ran, rann
rabat, rabbet, rabbit, rabid, rarebit
rabbi, rabi
rabbis, rabies
rabbit see rabat
rabi see rabbi
rabid see rabat
rabies see rabbis
raccoon, racon, rockoon
race, rais, raise, rase, rays, raze,
    res see also ras
RACHEL
rachet, rocket, roquet, roquette
rachis, rakes
rack, wrack
racks, rax, wracks
racon see raccoon
racy, razee
rad see raad
radar, rahdar
raddle, ratel, rattle, rotl
radial, radiale
radiance, radiants
radical, radicle
radish, reddish
raff, raffe, raft
rage, raj
raggee, raja, rajah
rah see Ra
rahdar see radar
raid, rayed
rail, rale
rain, reign, rein, rhein, Rhine,
    rind
rains, reigns, reins
rainy, rani
raion, rayon, rejon
rais see race
raise see race
raised, rased, razed

136

raiser, rasure, razer, razor
raj see rage
raja see ragee
rajah see raggee
rakes see rachis
raki, Reki
rale see rail
rami, ramie
ramous, ramus
ran see raan
ranch, ranche, wrench
rancor, ranker
randem, random
rani see rainy
ranker see rancor
rann see raan
RANNYS
rap, wrap
raphe, Raphia
rapped, rapt, wrapped
rapper, wrapper
rapport, report
rapt see rapped
raptor, rapture
rarebit see rabat
ras, rasse, wrasse see also race
rase see race
rased see raised
rasse see ras
rasure see raiser
ratch, retch, wretch
rate, ret, rete
ratel see raddle
rath, rathe, wraith, wrath, writhe,
    wroth
rational, rationale
ratine, ratoon, rattan, ratteen see
    also retain
rattle see raddle
raucous, Roccus
rauk, roc, rock, Rok, roque
raven, ravin, ravine, raving
rax see racks
ray, RE, reh, rey, rhea/Rhea, ri, RIG
rayed see raid
rayon see raion
rays see race
raze see race
razed see raised

137

razee *see* racy
razer *see* raiser
razor *see* raiser
RE *see* ray
READ, red, redd, rede, reed
ready, Reddi, reedy, rete
reaks, reeks
real, reel, rial, riel, rill, riyal
ream, riem, rim
REASON, resin *see also* resin *under
 separate listing*
reave, reeve, reive
REBEL
recede, reseed
receipt, recept, recipe, reseat *see
 also* recit
recent, resent *see also* rescind
recept *see* receipt
reciding, reciting, residing
recipe *see* receipt
recit, recite, reside *see also* receipt
reciting *see* reciding
reck, wreck *see also* reek
recked, wrecked
reckon, requin
recks, rex, wrecks
reclaim, reclame
recollect, recollet
RECORD
RECOUNT
recurrence, reoccurrence
red *see* read
redd *see* read
Reddi *see* ready
reddish *see* radish
rede *see* read
redoubt, redout
reducer, reductor
reed *see* READ
reedy *see* ready
reef, reif
reefer, refer
reek, wreak
reeks *see* reaks
reel *see* real
reest, wrist
reeve *see* reave
refel, REFILL, riffle
refer *see* reefer
reference, referents, reverence

138

referent, reverend, reverent
referents see reference
refill see refel
reflect, reflet
REFORM
REFUND
REFUSE
regal, regale, regle, riegel
regence, regency, regents
regimen, REGIMENT
register, registrar, registrer
regle see regal
reh see ray
reif see reef
reign see rain
reigns see rains
rein see rain
reins see rains
reiter, rider, ryder, writer
reive see reave
reiver, river, riviére, riviera/
    Riviera
reivers, revers, reverse, rivers
REJECT
rejoinder, rejoindure
rejon see raion
Reki see raki
relater, relator
RELAY
relic, relict
remain, reman, remand, remend
remanence, remnants
remanent, remnant
remark, remarque
remediable, remedial
remend see remain
remise, remiss see also amice
remitter, remittitur
remnant see remanent
remnants see remanence
rencontre, rencounter
rend, wren
renin, rennin
rent, rente, riant
renter, rentier
rents, rinse
RENVERSE
reoccurrence see recurrence
repartee, repertoire, repertory

repass, repast
repeal, repel
repeater, repetiteur
repel see repeal
repertoire see repartee
repetiteur see repeater
report see rapport
repertory see repartee
REPRISE
reproof, reprove
requin see reckon
res see race
rescind, resend see also recent
reseat see receipt
reseau, resew, resow
reseed see recede
resend see rescind
resent see recent
resew see reseau
reside see recit
residence, residents
residing see reciding
resin, rhason, ricin, rosin see
    also reason
resister, resistor
resow see reseau
respectably, respectfully,
    respectively
respond, responde
rest, wrest
RESUME
ret see rate
RETAIL, retell
retain, retene see also ratine
retch see ratch
rete see rate and ready
retell see RETAIL
retene see retain
retina, rytina
retract, retraict
RETREAT
reveal, reveil see also reveille
revealer, reveler
reveil see reveal
reveille, revel, revelry, reveree,
    reverie see also reveal
reveler see revealer
revelry see reveille
reveree see reveille

reverence _see_ reference
reverend _see_ referent
reverent _see_ referent
reverie _see_ reveille
revers _see_ reivers
reverse _see_ reivers
review, revue
REVISE
reviver, revivor
revue _see_ review
REWIND
REWRITE
rex _see_ recks
rey _see_ ray
rhamnose, Rhamnus
rhason _see_ resin
rhea/Rhea _see_ ray
rhein _see_ rain
rheum, room _see also_ rhm
Rhine _see_ rain
rhm, rhomb, rhumb, rum _see also_ rheum
rho, roe, ROW
rhodeose, rodeos
Rhodes, roads
rhodinal, rhodinol
rhoeo, rio
rhomb _see_ rhm
Rhone, roan, rone
rhos, roes, rose, ROWS
rhumb _see_ rhm
rhyme, rime, ryme
ri _see_ ray
rial _see_ real
riant _see_ rent
riband, ribbon, ribboned
rice, rise, ryes
ricer, riser, rizzar
ricin _see_ resin
riddel, riddle
rider _see_ reiter
riegel _see_ regal
riel _see_ real
riem _see_ ream
riff, rift
riffle _see_ refel
rifle, rival, rivel
rift _see_ riff
RIG _see_ ray
rigger, rigor

141

right, rite, wright/Wright, write
right off, write off
rigor see rigger
rile, ryal
rill see real
rim see ream
rime see rhyme
rind see rain
ring, wring
ringer, wringer
rinse see rents
rio see rhoeo
riot, ryot
ripe, rype
rise see rice
riser see ricer
risk, risqué
RISSOLE
rit, writ
rite see right
rithe, writhe
rival see rifle
rivel see rifle
river see reiver
rivers see reivers
riviera/Riviera see reiver
rivière see reiver
riyal see real
rizzar see ricer
road, rode, rowed
roads see Rhodes
roam, rom, Rome
roan see Rhone
roar, roer, rower
robber, rober, robur
roc see rauk
Roccus see raucous
rock see rauk
rocket see rachet
rockoon see raccoon
rode see road
rodeos see rhodeose
roe see rho
roer see roar
roes see rhos
roil, royal
roily, royally
Rok see roc
role, roll, rowel

rom see roam
romaine, Roman
Rome see roam
rondeau, rondo
rondel, rondelle, roundel
rondelet, roundelay, roundelet,
     rundlet
rondelle see rondel
rondo see rondeau
rone see Rhone
rood, rude, rued
rockie, rooky
room see rheum
roomer, rumor
roose, rouse, rues, ruse, Russ see
     also rhos and see rouse under
     separate listing
root, rout, route
roque see rauk
roquet see rachet
roquette see rachet
rose see rhos
rosel, rosella, roselle
roset, rosette
rosin see resin
rote, wrote
rotl see raddle
roton, rotund
roue, roux, rue
Rouen, ruin, rune
rough, ruff
roundel see rondel
roundelay see rondelet
roundelet see rondelet
rouse, ROWS see also rhose and
     roose
rout see root
route see root
roux see roue
ROW see rho
rowan, rowen
rowed see road
rowel see role
rowen see rowan
rower see roar
ROWS see rhos and rouse
royal see roil
royally see roily
rubber, rubor see also robber

143

rud, rudd see also rood
rude see rood
ruddy, ruttee, rutty
rue see roue
rued see rood
rues see roose
ruff see rough
ruin see Rouen
rum see rhm
rumor see roomer
rundlet see rondelet
rune see Rouen
rung, wrung
ruse see roose
rusell, russel, Russell
rushee, rushy
rusot, russet
Russ see roose
russel see rusell
Russell see rusell
russet see rusot
ruttee see ruddy
rutty see ruddy
ryal see rile
ryder see reiter
rye, wry
ryes see rice
ryme see rhyme
ryot see riot
rype see ripe
rytina see retina

S

s see ess
Saar see czar
Sabal, sable
Sabbat, Sabbath, sabot
saber, sabir
SABIA
sabin/Sabin, Sabine
sabir see saber
sable see Sabal
sabot see sabbat
sac, sack, sacque
saccharin, saccharine
saccular, secular
sachet, sashay
sack see sac

sacks, sax
sacque see sac
sacrad, sacred
sadder, saeter, satire, satyr, seder,
    setier see also cedar
sade, SAID, sayyid, seid, tsade
saeter see sadder
safar, safer
safe, seif
safer see safar
Sagai, sagair
SAID see sade
sail see cell
sailer, sailor
sailfish, selfish
sailor see sailer
saim, same
sain, sane, Seine
saith, saithe
Saiva, Siva
SAKE, Saki
sal, salle
salaam see salami
salary see celery
sale see cell
salep, saloop
Salinella, salinelle
salle see sal
sallee, sally/Sally
salmon see psammon
salon, saloon
saloop see salep
salter see psalter
saltery see psaltery
salvage, selvage
salver, salvor
same see saim
sample see ensample
sanatorium, sanitarium, sanitorium
sanatory, sanitary
sandhi, sandy
sands, sans
sandy see sandhi
sane see sain
sang, sangh
sank see cinque
sanitary see sanatory
sanitarium see sanatorium
sanitorium see sanatorium

sans _see_ sands
sapience, sapiens
sapor, sapper
sara, sarah/Sarah _see also_ sari
Saracen _see_ ceresin
sarah/Sarah _see_ sara
sarcel, sarcelle
sarcophagous, sarcophagus
sardine, sordine, sourdine
sarge, sorge
sari, serai, serry _see also_ sauri
    and sara
sarrazin _see_ ceresin
sarsen, sarson _see also_ ceresin
sart, sort
sash, seiche
sashay _see_ sachet
sassy, saucy
sat, sate, set, sit
Satan, sateen, satin _see also_ satine´
sate _see_ sat
sateen _see_ Satan
satellite, stellite
satin ,_see_ Satan
satine´, satinay, satiny _see also_
    Satan
satire _see_ sadder
saturnian/Saturnian, saturnine
satyr _see_ sadder
saucy _see_ sassy
saurel, sorel, sorrel, zoril
saury, soiree, sorry, sory _see_
    ,_also_ sari
sauté, sotie
saver, savior, savor
sawder, solder
say, sei
sayyid _see_ sade
sax _see_ sacks
scald, skald
scalar, scaler, scalor
scalpel, scapel, schepel
scary, skerry
scat, scatt
scatological _see_ eschatological
scatt _see_ scat
scaup, scoop, scop, scope, scoup,
    scup

scend, sen, send, sin see also
    scene
scene, seen see also scend
scenery, senary
scenical see cynical
scent see cent
scents see cens
schelling, shelling
schelly, Shelley, shelly
schema, schima
schepel see scalpel
schima see schema
schizogenous, schizogonous
schnorrer, snorer
sciara, sierra/Sierra
scilla see psylla
scion see cyan
scirrhous see ceras
scirrhus see ceras
scissel see cecil
scissile see cecil
scissure see Caesar
Sciurus see ceras
sclerose, sclerous
scoop see scaup
scoot, scute
scop see scaup
scope see scaup
scoup see scaup
scrae, scray, scree
scrapie, scrappy, scrapy
scray see scrae
scree see scrae
screeve, scrieve see also scribe
screws, scruze
scribe, scrive see also screeve
scrieve see screeve
scrive see scribe
scrooge/Scrooge, scrouge
scruze see screws
scull, skull
sculptor, sculpture
scup see scaup
scute see scoot
Scylla see pyslla
scyth, scythe
Scythia, Zythia
sea see c
sea-born, seaborne

seal see ceil
sealed see ceil
sealing see ceiling
seam, seem
seaman, seamen, semen
seamy, semé
sear see cere
searce see Circe
seas see cease
season, seisin
seasonable, seasonal
seau, sew, so, soe, soh, SOW
seave, sieve
secant, second, seconde, secondo,
    secund
secede, succeed
secle, sicel, sickle see also cycle
second see secant
seconde see secant
secondo see secant
secret, secrete
secretary, secretory
secrete see secret
secretin, secretion
secretory see secretary
sects, sex
secular see saccular
secund see secant
seder see sadder
see see c
seed see cede
seeder see cedar
seedy see cedi
seek, sic, sick, Sikh
seel see ceil
seeling see ceiling
seely, silly
seem see seam
seemly, semele/Semele, simile
seen see scene
seep see cepe
seer see cere
sees see cease
sei see say
seiche see sash
seid see sade
seidel, sidle
seif see safe

seigneur, seignior, senhor,
    senior, signor
Seine see sain
seisin see season
seize see cease
seizer see Caesar
seizor see Caesar
seizure see Caesar
sel see cell
selfish see sailfish
sell see cell
sellar see cellar
seller see cellar
selvage see salvage
semantic, sematic
semé see seamy
semeion, Simeon, simian
semele/Semele see seemly
semen see seaman
SEMIS
semple, simple
sempre, simper
sen see scend
senary see scenery
senate, sennet, sennit
send see scend
sender see cendre
Senegal see cingle and cynical
senhor see seigneur
senior see seigneur
sennet see senate
sennit see senate
sense see cens
senser see ceinture
senses see census
sensive see censive
senso see censo
sensor see ceinture
sensorial see censorial
sensual see censual
sent see cent
sentence, sentience
sentry see centaury
SEPARATE
sepulcher, sepulture
sequence, sequents, sequins
serac see ceric
serai see sari
seral see cereal

149

seraph, serif
seraphim, xerafin
serate see cerate
Sercial see cercal
sere see cere
serein see cerin
serene see cerin
serf, surf
serge, surge see also sarge
serial see cerial
seriate see cerate
sericin see ceresin
series see ceras
serif see seraph
serin see cerin
serine see cerin
serious see ceras
serous see ceras
serrate see cerate
serry see sari
service see Cervus
sesame, Sesamia
session see cession
sessionary see cessionary
sessor see cesser
seston see ceston
set see sat
setaceous see cetaceous
setal see cetyl
setier see sadder
seton/Seton see cetane
settee, sooty, suttee
setter, siddur, sitar, sitter
settler, settlor
seugh, shook, shuck
seven see cevine
sever, severe
sew see seau
sewage, sewerage
sewer, suer see also shirr
sewerage see sewage
sewn, sone
sex see sects
sexed, sext
sextant, sexton
sferics, spherics
shack see chack
shad see Chad
shaft see chaft

shagreen see chagrin
shah see pshaw
shake, sheik see also cheek
shale, shall, shell
sham see cham
shammes, shams, shamus
shanty see chantey
shard see chard
share see chair
sharif, sheriff
sharki, sharky
sharpie see charpie
shary see chary
shaw/Shaw see pshaw
shay see chace
she, shea, Shia see also chace
shear, sheer see also chare and
     shirr
sheath, sheathe
sheen, shin
sheep, ship
sheer see shear
sheik see cheek and shake
shelf, shelve
shell see shale
Shelley see schelly
she'll, shill
shelling see schelling
shelly see schelly
shelve see shelf
sheriff see sharif
sherry see chary
shew see CHOU
Shia see she
shicker, shikar
shier, shire, shyer
shik see cheek
shikar see shicker
shikken see chicken
shill see she'll
shin see sheen
ship see sheep
shire see shier
shirr, shoer, sure see also sewer
shoal, shole
shock see chock
shoe see CHOU
shoer see shirr
shole see shoal

shone, shown
shoo see CHOU
shook see seugh
shoot see chute
shor, shore see also shirr
shot see chott
shou, show, shu see also CHOU
shown see shone
shows see chausses
shu see shou and CHOU
shuck see seugh
shudder, shutter
shut see chute
shutter see shudder
shyer see shier
si see c
sial, sile
Sibyl see cebell
sic see seek
sicel see cycle
Sicily see cicely
Sicilian see caecilian
sick see seek
sickle see secle
siddur see setter
side, sighed
sider see cider
sideral, sidereal
sidle see seidel
sie see psi
Siena, sienna
sierra/Sierra see sciara
sieve see seave
sigh see psi
sighed see side
sighs see psis
sight see cite
sign see cyan
signate see cygnet
signet see cygnet
signor see seigneur
Sikh see seek
sil see ceil
sild see ceil
sile see sial
silence, silents
Silicea see Cilicea
sill see ceil
silly see seely

sima see cyma
Simeon see semeion
simian see semeion
similar, simular
simile see seemly
simper see sempre
simple see semple
simular see similar
sin see scend
since see cens
sine see cyan
sing, singe, Singh, Synge
singeing, singing
Singh see sing
singing see singeing
single see cingle
Sinicism see cynicism
sink see cinque
sinter see centare
Sion see cyan
Sioux, sou, sous, sue/Sue
sipe see cepe
sir, sur
siris see ceras
sirrah, sura, surah, surra
sisal see cecil/Cecil
sisel see cecil/Cecil
Sistine see cysteine
Sisyphus, ziziphus
sit see sat
sitar see setter
site see cite
sits, sitz
sitter see setter
sitz see sits
Siva see Saiva
sizar see cicer
size see psis
sizer see cicer
skald see scald
skean, skein, skene
skee, ski
skeet, skete
skein see skean
sken, skin
skene see skean
skerry see scary
skete see skeet
ski see skee
skin see sken

skin a flint, skinflint
skull see scull
sky, Skye see also skee
slade, slayed
slander, slender
SLAVER, sliver, slobber, slumber
slay, sleigh, sley
slayed see slade
sleave, sleeve
sleek, slick
sleeve see sleave
sleigh see slay
sleight, slight
slender see slander
slew, SLOUGH, slue
sley see slay
slick see sleek
slight see sleight
slipe, slype
sliver see SLAVER
slobber see SLAVER
sloe, slow see also slew
SLOUGH see slew
slow see sloe
slue see slew
slumber see SLAVER
slype see slipe
smelled, smelt
smellie, smelly
smelt see smelled
smooch, smouch, smudge, smutch
snail, snell
snark, snork
snell see snail
snoek, snook
snoose, snooze
snorer see schnorrer
snork see snark
so see seau
soak, soke
soaker, sokhor
soar, sore, sowar, sower
soared, sword
sober, Sobor
soe see seau
soh see seau
soiree see saury
soke see soak
sokhor see soaker

154

sol, sole, soul
solace, solus
solar, soler
sold, soled, souled
solder see sawder
sole see sol
SOLEA
soled see sold
solen, solion, solon
soler see solar
solidary, solitaire, solitary
solion see solen
solitaire see solidary
solitary see solidary
solon see solen
solus see solace
soma, somma, suma, summa
some, Somme, soum, sum
somma see soma
Somme see some
son, sun, sunn
sone see sewn
sonny, sunni, sunny
soop, soup
soot, suet, suit, suite, sute see also
    suite under separate listing
sooter, souter, suiter, suitor
sooth, soothe
sooty see settee
sorceress, sorcerous
sordine see sardine
sore see soar
sorel see saurel
sorge see sarge
sorosis see cirrhosis
sorrel see saurel
sorrow, zorrow, zorra
sorry see saury
sort see sart
sory see saury,
sotie see saute
sou see Sioux
soul see sol
souled see sold
soum see some
soup see soop
sourdine see sardine
sous see Sioux
souter see sooter
souverain, sovereign

155

SOW see seau
sowar see soar
sower see soar
spade, spayed
spae, spay, SPET
spale, spell
Sparassis, sparaxis
spay see spae
spayed see spade
spear, speer
speciality, specialty
specks, specs
speel, spiel, spill see also spial
speer see spear
speider, spider
speiss, spice
spell see spale
spend, spin
SPET see spae
spheral, spherical
spherics see sferics
spial, spile see also speel
spice see speiss
spider see speider
spiel see speel
spile see spial
spill see speel
spin see spend
spinal, spinel
spinner, spinor
spiral, spirale
spiritous, spirituous, spiritus
     see also spiritual
spirit, spirt, sprit, sprite see
     also esprit
spiritual, spirituel
spirituous see spiritous
spiritus see spiritous
spirt see spirit
spital, spittle
sponsion, sponson
spoor, spore
spraing, sprang
spreeuw, sprue
sprent, sprint
sprit see spirit
sprite see spirit
spruce, sprues
sprue see spreeuw

sprues see spruce
squadder, squatter
squaller, squalor
squatter see squadder
squdgy, squeegee
squeal, squill
squeegee see squdgy
squill see squeal
squirl, squirrel
STABILE, stable, staple
stade, staid, stayed
stain, stane
stair, stare, stayer
stairs, stares, stayers
stake, steak
stalactite, stalagmite
staler, stelar, stellar
stamen, stamin
stane see stain
staple see STABILE
stare see stair
stares see stairs
starlet, sterlet
starlight, starlite
stater, stator
stationary, stationery
stator see stater
statue, stature, statute
stayed see stade
stayer see stair
stayers see stairs
steady, study, sturdy
steak see stake
steal, steel, stele, still
stean, steen, stein
steel see steal
steely, stele, stilly
steen see stean
steer, stere
stein see stean
stelar see staler
stele see steely and steal
stellar see staler
stelletta, stellite, stiletto
stent, stint
stenter, stentor
step, steppe
stere see steer
stereome, stereum

157

stereoptican, stereopticon
stereotype, stereotypy
stereum see stereome
sterile, sterol
sterlet see starlet
sterol see sterile
stich, stick, stitch
sticks, Styx
stile, style
stiletto see stelletta
still see steal
stilly see steely
STINGY
stint see stent
stipel, stipple, stipule
stirp, stirrup, stir-up
stirps, stirrups
stirrup see stirp
stirrups see stirps
stir-up see stirp
stitch see stich
stoat, stoit
stoep, stoop, stop, stoup, stupe,
    stupp
stoit see stoat
stolen, stollen, stolon
stood, stud see also stade
stoop see stoep
stop see stoep
storey, story
stoup see stoep
stour, stower
straight, strait
straighten(ed) see straiten(ed)
strait see straight
straiten(ed) see straighten(ed)
strake, streak, streek
strap, strop
stratous, stratus
streak see strake
streek see strake
strider, stridor
strop see strap
stud see stood
studding, studying
study see steady
studying see studding
stumble, stummel
stupe see stoep

stupp see stoep
sturdy see steady
sty, stye
stylar, styler
style see stile
styler see stylar
styrol, styryl
Styx see sticks
SUBJECT
SUBLEASE
SUBORDINATE
subsidiary, subsidy
subtile, subtle, sutile, suttle
subtler, suttler
succeed see secede
succent, succinct
succor, sucker, sucre
succubous, succubus
suck, sulk, suk
sucker see succor
sucre see succor
sudds, suds
sue/Sue see Sioux
suede, swade, swayed, Swede
suer see sewer
suet see soot
suit see soot
suite, sweet see also soot
suiter see sooter
suitor see sooter
suk see suck
sulfenyl, sulfinyl
sulfonal, sulfonyl
sulfureous, sulfurous
sulk see suck
sultan, sultane
sum see some
suma see soma
suman, sumen
summa see soma
summary, summery
summoner, sumner/Sumner
summery see summary
sumner/Sumner see summoner
sun see son
sunck, sunk
sundae, Sunday
sundri, sundry
sunk see sunck

sunn see son
sunni see sonny
sunny see sonny
super, supra
superciliary, supercilious,
    supraciliary
superconscious, supraconscious
superintendence, superintendents
supernormal, supranormal
SUPPLEMENT
supplemental, supplementary
supplicat, supplicate
supposititious, supposititious
supra see super
supraciliary see superciliary
supraconscious see superconscious
supranormal see supernormal
SUPREME
sur see sir
sura see sirrah
surah see sirrah
SURCEASE see Cercis
surculus see circulus
sure see shirr and suer
surf see serf
surge see serge
suricate, surrogate
Surinam, surname
surplice, surplus
surra see sirrah
surrogate see suricate
SURVEY
susan/Susan, susian/Susian
susurrous, susurrus
sute see soot
sutile see subtile
sutler see subtler
suttee see settee
suttle see subtile
suttler see subtler
svelt, swelt
swade see suede
swale, swell see also sweal
swallo, swallow
swat, swats, swot
swath, swathe
swats see swat
swayed see suede
sweal, sweel, swill see also swale

Swede see suede
sweel see sweal
sweet see suite
swell see swale
swelt see svelt
swill see sweal
swing, swinge
SWINGER, zwinger
sword see soared
swot see swat
syce see psis
sycosis see psychosis
sye see psi
syenite see cyanide
Sylphon, sylvan
symbolist see cembolist
symbol see cymbal
symmetry see cemetery
sync see cinque
syne see cyan
synema see cinema
Synge see sing
syntaxis, syntexis
Syrian, Zyrian
syssel see cecil
systematic, systemic
Szi see c

T

t, te, tea, tee, ti, tiu
Taal, tael, tail, taille, tale,
    tall, Tayal, tell
Tabalian, tabellion
tabber, tabor
tabbies, tabes
tabellion see Tabalian
tabes see tabbies
tabor see tabber
taboret, tabret
tabulator, tabulatur
tacet, tacit, tasset
TACHE
tacit see tacet
tacked, tact, takt
tacks, tax
tact see tacked
tael see Taal
taeniada, taenidea

161

tahr, tar, tawer, tor, torr
tahsil, tassel
Tai, Thai, tie, tye, tyee, Tyigh
tail see Taal
taille see Taal
tailleur, tailor, teller
tait, tate, tête
taken, takin
takt see tacked
talc, talk
tale see Taal
taler, taller
talk see talc
talkie, talky, tawkee
tall see Taal
taller see taler
Tamar, tamer, tammar see also tamber
tamber, tambor, tambour see also
    Tamar
tamer see Tamar
tamis, tammy
tammar see Tamar
tammy see tamis
tangale, tangle
TANGI, tangy
tangle see tangale
tangy see TANGI
tao see dhow
taper, tapir
tar see tahr
tarantella, tarantula
tarboosh, tarbush
tare, TEAR, TIER, Tyr see also
    tire
tari, TARRY, terry/Terry
tarrier, terrier
TARRY see tari
tart, tort see also torta
tartar, Tatar, tater, tatter, totter
tartarous, Tartarus
tass, tasse
tassel see tahsil
tasset see tacet
Tatar see tartar
tate see tait
tater see tartar
tatou, tatoo, TATU
tatter see tartar
tattoo see tatou

TATU see tatou
taught, taut, tout
tau, taw, tow see also dhow
taupe, tope
Tauri, tori, torii, tory/Tory
Taurus, torose, torus
taut see taught
taw see tau
tawer see tahr
tawie, toy see also toey
tawkee see talkie
tax see tacks
taxer, taxor
taxes, taxus/Taxus, texas/Texas
taxor see taxer
taxus/Taxus see taxes
Tayal see Taal
tayra, tiara
te see t
tea see t
teal, teil, til, till
team, teem
TEAR see tare
teas, tease, tees, Tees
tee see t
teem see team
teen see ctene
tees/Tees see teas
teeter, titar, titter
Tehran see pteron and terrain
teil see teal
teind, tend
tell see Taal
teller see tailleur
ten, tin
tenant, tenet
tend see teind
tender, tendre, tinder
tenderness, tendresse
tendre see tender
tendresse see tenderness
tenet see tenant
tenne, tinny
tenner, tenor, tenure
tense, tents
tenser, tensor
tensile, tinsel
tension, tenson
tensor see tenser

tent, tint
tents see tense
tenuis, tenuous
tenure see tenner
tepee, tippee, tippy
terce, terse, tierce, turse
termen, termine, termon, termone
termer, termor
termine see termen
termon see termen
termone see termen
termor see termer
tern, terne, turn
ternar, tourneur, tournure,
    turner/Turner
terne see tern
terpin, terrapin
terrace see pteris
terrain, terrane, terrene, terrine,
    terron, train, tureen, turin/
    Turin, turion see also pteron
terrapin see terpin
terrar, terrier, terror see also
    tarrier
terrene see terrain
terrier see tarrier and terrar
terrine see terrain
terron see pteron and terrain
terror see terrar and tarrier
terry/Terry see tari
terse see terce
testae, testee, testy
tête see tait
tetragenous, tetragynous
tetramine, tetrammine
tetrapteran, tetrapteron
tetrapterous, tetrapterus
tetrastichous, tetrastichus
tetrazene, tetrazine
tew, to, too, tui, two see also t
texas/Texas see taxes
textual, textural
Thai see Tai
THAIS, thighs
thallous, thallus
than, thane, then, thin
the, thee
theave, thief, thieve
thee see the

164

thee's, the's, these, this
their, there, there're, they're
    thir
theirs, there's, thyrse
them, theme
then see than
theocracy, theocrasy
there see their
therefor, therefore
there're see their
there's see theirs
therm, thurm
the's see thee's
these see thee's
theses, thesis
they're see their
thick, thik
thief see theave
thigh, thy
thighs see THAIS
thik see thick
thin see than
thir see their
thirl, thurl
this see thee's
thorough, threw, through, thru
thos, those
thrash, thresh
threw see thorough
thrice, trice
thrill, trill
thriller, triller
thrilling, trilling
throe, throw
throes, throws
thrombin, thrombon
throne, thrown
through see thorough
throw see throe
thrown see throne
throws see throes
thru see thorough
thruster, thrustor
THULE
thurl see thirl
thurm see therm
thy see thigh
thyme, time
thumol, thymyl

165

```
thyrse see theirs
ti see t
tiara see tayra
tic, tick
tical, tickle
tick see tic
ticker, tikor, tiqueur
tickle see tical
tickling, tikling
tidal, title, tittle
tiddly, tidley
tide, tied
tidley see tiddly
tidy, tydie
tie see Tai
tied see tide
TIER see tare
tierce see terce
tiff, tift
tig, tyg
tighter, titer
tikor see ticker
tikling see tickling
til see teal
till see teal
timar, timer
timber, timbre
time see thyme
timer see timar
timpani, typany
tin see ten
tincal, tinchel, tinkle
tinder see tender
tinkle see tincal
tinny see tenne
tinsel see tensile
tint see tent
tip, typp
tippee see tepee
tippy see tepee
tiqueur see ticker
tirak, track
tire, Tyr, Tyre
tirr, tur
'tis, see its
tisane see ptisan
titar see teeter
titer see tighter
TITI
```

title see tidal
tittle see tidal
titter see teeter
tiu see t
tjanting see chanting
to see tew
toad, toed, towed
toady, tody
tocsin, toxin
tody see toady
toe, tow
toed see toad
toey, towhee, towie see also tawie
toil, toile
toilet, toilette
toise, toys
told, tolled
tole, toll see also told
tolled see told
tomb, tome, toom
TON, tun
tong, tongue
tonight, tonite
too see tew
tool, tule, tulle see also tuille
toom see tomb
toon, tune
toona, tuna
tooter, Tudor, tutor
tope see taupe
tor see tahr
tora, Torah
TORE, TOWER
tori see Tauri
toric, torque
torii see Tauri
tornada, tornado
torose see Taurus
torque see toric
torr see tahr
tort see tart
torta, torte see also tart
tortious, tortoise, tortuous,
    torturous
torus see Taurus
tory/Tory see Tauri
totter see tarter
tough, tuff
tourelle, tourill

tournee, tourney
tourneur see ternar
tourney see tournee
tournure see ternar
tout see taught
tow see toe and tau
towed see toad
TOWER see TORE
towhee see toey
towie see toey
toxin see tocsin
toy see tawie
toys see toise
trachycarpous, trachycarpus
track see tirak
tracked, tract
trader, traitor
trail, trial, triol
train see terrain
traipse, traps
traitor see trader
TRANSFER
TRANSFORM
transience, transiens, transients
transmontane, transmundane
TRANSPORT
traps see traipse
travail, travel
trave, TREF
travel see travail
travis/Travis, travois, travoy
tray, trey
TREEN
TREF see trave
trendel, trendle, trental, trindle
trew, true
trews, truce
trey see tray
tri, try
trial see trail
trice see thrice
Trieste, triste, tryst
trill see thrill
triller see thriller
trilling see thrilling
trimer, trimmer
trindle see trendel
triodion, triodon
triol see trail

triply, Tripoli, tripylea
triste see Trieste
trivet, trivvet
troche, trochee
troll, trull
trolley, trolly
trollop, trollope/Trollope
trolly see trolley
troolie, truly
troop, trope, troupe
trophi, trophy
trotter, trotteur
trottie, trotty
trough, trow
troupe see troop
trouse, trows
trow see trough
trowie, troy/Troy
trows see trouse
troy/Troy see trowie
truce see trews
true see trew
trull see troll
truly see troolie
truss, trust
trustee, trusty
truster, trustor
trusty see trustee
try see tri
trygon, try gun
tryst see Trieste
tsade see sade
tubbie, tubby
tubulous, tubulus
tucks, tux
Tudor see tooter
tuff see tough
tui see tew
tuille, tweel, twill, 'twill
    see also tool
tule see tool
tulip see julep
tulle see tool
tun see TON
tuna see toona
tune see toon
tur see tirr
turban, turbine
turbit, turbot

tureen see terrain
turin/Turin see terrain
turion see terrain
turkey/Turkey, turki
turn see tern
turner/Turner see ternar
turnip, turnup, turn up
turse see terce
tusch, tusche, tush
tussal, tussle
tutor see tooter
tuttie see tutee
tutty see tutee
tux see tucks
twaddell, twaddle
tweed, tweet, twit
tweel see tuille
tween, twin
tweet see tweed
twill see tuille
'twill see tuille
twin see tween
twit see tweed
two see tew
tydie see tidy
tye see Tai
tyee see Tai
tyg see tig
Tyigh see Tai
Tylosaurus, Tylosurus
tympany see timpani
typhous, typhus
typp see tip
Tyr see tare and tire
Tyre see tire
Tyranni, tyranny, Tyrrheni
tyrannis, tyrannous, tyrannus
tyranny see Tyranni
tyrolean/Tyrolean,
     tyrolienne/Tyrolienne
Tyrrheni see Tyranni

U

u see ewe
uca, yucca see also yeuky
udder, utter
ugli, ugly
uhlan, yulan

uke, yeuk, yuk
ultramontane, ultramundane
ultra vires, ultravirus
umbel see humble
umber see hombre
umbre see hombre
unalike, unlike
unapt see inapt
uncal, uncial, uncle, unco
uncensored, uncensured
uncial see uncal
uncle see uncal
unco see uncal
UNDERGROUND
under way, underway, under weigh
undine see ondine
undo, undue
unexceptionable, unexceptional
unexercised, unexorcised
ungenteel, ungentle
ungird, ungirt
unicom, unicum
uniparous, uniporous
unlade, unlaid
unlike see unalike
unreal, unreel
unreave, unreeve
unreel see unreal
unreeve see unreave
unseal, unseel
unstaid, unstayed
unwanted, unwonted
upon, up on
uprisal see appraisal
ur/Ur see err and ear
uranous, Uranus, urinous
uranyl, urinal
urban, urbane
urd see erred
urea, uria, Uriah
uric, Yurak. Yurok, Yuruk
urinal see uranyl
urinous see uranous
urn see earn
usar, user, usurer
USE see ewes
user see usar
usurer see usar
Ute, yuit
util, utile

utter *see* udder

V

v, vee
vaal, vail, VALE, veal, veil
vag, vague
vagal, vagile
vague *see* vag
vai, vie
vail *see* vaal
vain, vane, vein
vair, var, vare
vaire, vari, vary, veery, very
valance, valence, valiance
VALE *see* vaal
valence *see* valance
valent, valiant
valet, vali, valley
valiance *see* valance
valiant *see* valent
valley *see* valet
valor, velour, velure
valse, vaults
valvate, velvet
vamper, vampire
vane *see* vain
vanillin, vanillon
vannal, veinule, venal, venial,
    vennel, venule *see* *also* vinal
vannus, veinous
vantage, ventage, vintage
var *see* vair
vare *see* vair
varec, variac
vari *see* vaire
variac *see* varec
variad, varied
varicose, verrucose
varies, various, varus, virose,
    virous, virus
varmeter, varminter
varus *see* varies
vary *see* vaire
vassal, vessel
vaults *see* valse
veal *see* vaal
vector, victor/Victor
Veda, Vedda

172

```
vee see v
veep, vip
veery see vairé
vega, viga, vigia
veil see vaal
vein see vain
veinous see vannus
veinule see vannal
vellum, velum
velour see valor
velum see vellum
velure see valor
velvet see valvate
vena, vina, vinea
venal see vannal
vender, venter, venture, vintner
venial see vannal
venison see benison
vennel see vannal
venose, venous, Venus
vent, vint
ventage see vantage
ventail, ventil, ventile see also
      vannal and vinal
venter see vender
ventil see ventail
ventile see ventail
venture see vender
venule see vannal
Venus see venose
veracious, voracious
veracity, voracity
verbal, verbile
verdure, verger
verner, vernier
verrucose see varicose
versed, verst
verses, versus
version, virgin
verst see versed
versus see verses
vertex, vortex
vertical, verticil, vortical
vervel, vervelle
very see vairé
vesical, vesicle
vessel see vassal
vest see invest
vial, vile, viol
```

173

vicaress, vicarious
VICE, VISE
victor/Victor see vector
Victorian, victorine
victual, viddhal, vital
victuals, vitals
viddhal see victual
vie see vai
viga see vega
vigia see vega
vila, villa
vile see vial
villa see vila
villain, villein
villanella, villanelle
villein see villain
villous, villus
vina see vena
vinal, vineal, vinyl see also
     vannal
vinea see vena
vineal see vinal
vinyl see vinal
vint see vent
vintage see vantage
vintner see vender
vinyl see vinal
viol see vial
VIOLA
violan, violin, violine, violone
VIOLATE, violet, violette
violin see violan
violine see violan
violone see violan
vip see veep
viral, virial, virile, virl
virgin see version
virial see viral
virile see viral
virl see viral
virose see varies
virous see varies
virtu, virtue
virus see varies
viscose, viscous, viscus
VISE see VICE
visit, visite
visor, vizier
vita, vitta
vital see victual

174

vitals see victuals
vitellin, vitelline
VITIATE
vitta see vita
viva, vive
vivandier, vivandière
vive see viva
viviparous, viviparus
vizier see visor
voder, voter
voe, voeu, vow
vogie, vogue
voiture, vultur, vulture
VOLE, volet
volutin, volution
volva, vulva
voracious see veracious
voracity see veracity
vortex see vertex
vortical see vertical
voter see voder
vow see voe
voyager, voyageur, voyeur
vulgar, vulgare
vultur see voiture
vulture see voiture
vulva see volva

W

wa, wah, waugh, waw
wack, wacke, whack
wacky, wahki
waddle, wattle
waddy, wadi
wade, weighed
wader, waiter
wadi see waddy
waesucks, Wessex
waf, waff
waggel, waggle
Wagner, wagoner
wah see wa
waif, waive, wave
wail, wale, well, whale see
    also weal
wailer, waler, weller, whaler
wails, Wales
wain, wane, Wayne

waist, waste
waister, waster
wait, weight
waiter see wader
waiting, weighting see also
    wedding
waive see waif
waiver, waver
wakhi see wacky
wale see wail
waler see wailer
Wales see wails
wali, wally, waly, whally
wall, waul, wawl
wallah, wallow
wallet, wallette
wally see wali
waly see wali
wan see one
wand see one
wander, wonder
wane see wain
wanes, wanze see also once
want, wont, won't
wants see once
wanze see once and wanes
wap, whap, whaup, wop
ward, warred
ware, wear, weir, we're, where
    see also were
warfarin, warfaring
wari, warree, wary, weary, wherry,
    whirry, wiry, worry see
    also wirra
Warli, whirley, whirly, whorly,
    wurley
warm, worm, wurm
warn, warren/Warren, worn
warrantee, warranty
warred see ward
warree see wari
warren/Warren see warn
wart, wert, whort, wort
wary see wari
waste see waist
waster see waister
WAT, watt/Watt, what, wot
water, watter
waterie, watery

176

watt/Watt see wat
watter see water
wattle see waddle
waugh see wa
waul see wall
wave see waif
waver see waiver
waw see wa
wawl see wall
wax, whacks
way, weigh, wey, whey see also away
Wayne see wain
we, wee, whee
weak, week, wick
weal, weel, we'll, wheal, wheel,
    will see also wail
weald, wheeled, wield, willed
wean, ween, wheen
weaner, wiener see also weiner
wear see ware
weary see wari
weasel, whistle
weather, wether, whether
weave, we've
weaver, weever
web, webb/Webb
we'd, weed, whid
wedding, wetting, whetting
    see also waiting
wedgie, wedgy
wee see we
weed see we'd
week see weak
weel see weal
ween see wean
weanie, weeny
weet, wheat
weever see weaver
weeze, wheeze, whiz, wiz
weigh see way
weighed see wade
weight see wait
weighting see waiting
weiner, whiner, whinner, winna,
    winner see also weaner
weir see ware
weld, welled
welder, weldor
welk, whelk

177

well _see_ wail
we'll _see_ weal
welled _see_ weld
weller _see_ wailer
welp, whelp
Welsh rabbit, Welsh rarebit
wem, whim
wen, when, whin, win _see also_ wend
wench, winch
wend, WIND _see also_ wen
wends, wens, whence, wince,
    WINDS, winze
wenny, whinny, winnie _see also_ whiny
wens _see_ wends
were, whir(r), wirr _see also_ ware
we're _see_ ware
wert _see_ wart
Wessex _see_ waesucks
wet, whet
wether _see_ weather
wetter, whetter
wetting _see_ wedding
we've _see_ weave
wey _see_ way
whack _see_ wack
whacks _see_ wax
whale _see_ wail
whaler _see_ wailer
whally _see_ wali
whamp, whomp, womp
whap _see_ wap
what _see_ wat
whaup _see_ wap
wheal _see_ weal
wheat _see_ weet
whee _see_ we
wheedle, whittle, wittol
wheel _see_ weal
wheeled _see_ weald
wheen _see_ wean
wheeze _see_ weeze
whelk _see_ welk
whelp _see_ welp
when _see_ wen
whence _see_ wends
where _see_ ware
wherefor, wherefore
wherrit, worrit
wherry _see_ wari

178

whet see wet
whether see weather
whetter see wetter
whetting see wedding
whew, woo
whewer, wooer
whey see way
which, wich, witch
whicker, wicker
WHIFFLER
whid see we'd
whidah, widow
Whig, wig
while, wild, wile
whiles, wilds, wiles
whim see wem
whin see wen
whine, wine
whiner see weiner
whinner see weiner
whinny see wenny
whiny, winey see also wenny
whir(r) see were
whirl, whorl, whurl, wirl, worl
whirled, world
whirley see Warli
whirly see Warli
whirr see were
whirry see wari
whirtle, whortle, wordle
WHISH, wish
whisht, wished
whisk, wisk
whist, wis, wist
whistle see weasel
whit, wit
white, wight, wite
whiten, witan
whither, wither see also weather
whitish, widish
whitling, whittling
whittle see wheedle
whittling see whitling
whiz see weeze
whoa, woe, wough
whole see hole
wholly see holey
whomp see whamp
whoop see hoop

whooper, whopper
whore see hoar
whored see hoard
whorer see horror
whorl see whirl
whorly see Warli
whort see wart
whortle see whirtle
whory see hoary
who's, whose
whurl see whirl
why, Wye, y
wich see which
wick see weak
wicked, wicket
wicker see whicker
wicket see wicked
widdy, witty
widish see whitish
widow see whidah
wield see weald
wiener see weaner
wig see Whig
wigan, wiggen
wiggle, wriggle
wight see white
wild see while
wilds see whiles
wile see while
wiles see whiles
wilkeite, Willkieite
will see weal
willed see weald
willie/Willie, willy/Willy
Willkieite see wilkeite
willy/Willy see willie/Willie
win see wen
wince see wends
winch see wench
WIND, wined, WYND see also wend
windlass, windless
winds see wends
wine see whine
wined see WIND
winey see whiny
winna see weiner
winner see weiner
winnie/Winnie see wenny
winze see wends

180

wirl _see_ whirl
wirr _see_ were
wirra, wirrah _see also_ wari
wiry _see_ wari
wis _see_ whist
wish _see_ WHISH
wished _see_ whisht
wisk _see_ whisk
wist _see_ whist
wistaria, wisteria
wit _see_ whit
witan _see_ whiten
witch _see_ which
wite _see_ white
with, withe
wither _see_ whither
wittol _see_ wheedle
witty _see_ widdy
witwall, woodwall
wiz _see_ weeze
woad, wold
wobbegong, woebegone
woe _see_ whoa
woebegone _see_ wobbegong
wold _see_ woad
wolf, wolve, woof
wolffish, wolfish
wolve _see_ wolf
womp _see_ whamp
won _see_ one
wonder _see_ wander
wont _see_ want
won't _see_ want
woo _see_ whew
wood, would, wud
woodwall _see_ witwall
wooer _see_ whewer
woof _see_ wolf
woold, wooled
woo-woo, wouwou
wop _see_ wap
wordie, wordy
wordle _see_ whirtle
worl _see_ whirl
world _see_ whirled
worm _see_ warm
worn _see_ warn
worrit _see_ wherret
worry _see_ wari

181

worst, wurst
wort see wart
wot see wat
wough see whoa
would see wood
WOUND
wouwou see woo-woo
wrack see rack
wracks see racks
wraith see rath
wrap see rap
wrapped see rapped
wrapper see rapper
wrasse see ras
wrath see rath
wreak see reek
wreath, wreathe
wreck see reck
wrecked see recked
wrecks see recks
wren see rend
wrench see ranch
wrest see rest
wretch see ratch
wriggle see wiggle
wright/Wright see right
wring see ring
wringer see ringer
wrist see reest
writ see rit
write see right
write off see right off
writer see reiter
writhe see rath and rithe
wrote see rote
wroth see rath
wrung see rung
wry see rye
wud see wood
wurley see Warli
wurm see warm
wurst see worst
Wye see why
WYND see WIND

                X

x see Aex
xanthene, xanthian, xanthin, xanthine

Xanthoria, Xanthorrhoea
xat see cat
xenodocheum, xenodochium
xerafin see seraphim
Xiphias, Ziphius
xiphioid, xiphoid, ziphioid
xurel see jewel
xylenol, xylenyl
xylol, xylyl

Y

y see why
yack, yak
yae, ye, yea
yahoo, yahu
yair, yare, year
yak see yack
Yale, yell see also ye'll
y'all, yawl
yankee, yanqui
yao, yaw
yap, yapp
yare see yair
yaud, yawed
yauld, yawled
yaw see yao
yawed see yaud
yawl see y'all
yawled see yauld
ye see yae
yea see yae
yean, yen, yin
year see yair
yeld, yelled
yell see Yale
ye'll, yill see also Yale
yelled see yeld
yen see yean
yet, yett
yeuk see uke
yeuky, Yuchi, Yuki see also uca
yew see ewe
yewen, yuan/Yuan
yews see ewes
yill see ye'll
yin see yean
ymir see emir
yod, yodh

yogh, yoke, yolk
yokol see jokul
yolk see yogh
yon, yond
you see ewe
you'll, yule
your see ewer
you're see ewer
yuan/Yuan see yewan
yucca see uca
Yuchi see yeuky
Yueh see ewe
yuit see Ute
yuk see uke
Yuki see yeuky
yulan see uhlan
yule see you'll
Yurak see uric
Yurok see uric
Yuruk see uric

Z

z, zea, zee/Zee
zabra, zebra
zaffer, zephyr
zea see z
zealous see jealous
zebra see zabra
Zebrina, zebrine
zee/Zee see z
zein, zen/Zen
ZEMI, zemmi, zimmi
zen/Zen see zein
zephyr see zaffer
zero see cero
zimmi see ZEMI
zingel see cingle
Zion see cyan
ziphioid see xiphioid
Ziphius see Xiphias
zither see cither
ziziphus see Sisyphus
zonda, Zonta
zone, zoon
Zonta see zonda
zoon see zone
zoozoo, zuzu
zoril see saurel

zorra _see_ sorrow
zorro _see_ sorrow
zuzu _see_ zoozoo
zwinger _see_ swinger
Zyrian _see_ Syrian
Zythia _see_ Scythia